QUESTIONS RELATING TO THE JINN MAGIC AND CONJURING

Shaykh Salih Al-Fawzan

ISBN: 978-1-5323-9995-4

First Edition: Jumādā al-'Ūlā 1440 A.H. / January 2019 C.E.

Cover Design: Usul Design
E-mail: info@usuldesign.com

Translator: Rasheed Barbee

Editing & Formatting: Razanah Gregory
Annurediting.com

Publisher's Information:
Authentic Statements Publishing
P. O. Box 15536
Philadelphia, PA. 19131
215.382.3382
215.382.3782-Fax

Store:
5000 Locust Street (Side Entrance)
Philadelphia, Pa 19139

Website: www.authenticstatements.com

E-mail: info@authenticstatements.com

Please visit our website for upcoming publications, audio/DVD online catalog, and info on events and seminars, insha Allāh.

Transliteration Table

Consonants

ء	'	د	d	ض	ḍ	ك	k
ب	b	ذ	dh	ط	ṭ	ل	l
ت	t	ر	r	ظ	ẓ	م	m
ث	th	ز	z	ع	ʿ	ن	n
ج	j	س	s	غ	gh	ه	h
ح	ḥ	ش	sh	ف	f	و	w
خ	kh	ص	ṣ	ق	q	ي	y

Vowels

Short	◌َ	a	◌ِ	i	◌ُ	u
Long	ـَا	ā	ـِي	ī	ـُو	ū
Diph-thongs	ـَي	ay	ـَو	aw		

Glyphs

- *Sallallāhu ʿalayhi wa sallam* (May Allāh's praise & salutations be upon him)
- *ʿAlayhis-salām* (Peace be upon him)
- *ʿAza wa jal* (Mighty and Majestic)
- *Radiyallāhu ʿanhu* (May Allāh be pleased with him)
- *Radiyallāhu ʿanhum* (May Allāh be pleased with them)

TABLE OF CONTENTS

بِسْمِ اللّـهِ الرَّحْمَـٰنِ الرَّحِيمِ

All praises belong to Allāh, the Lord of all that exists, the Most Beneficent, and the Most Merciful of those who show mercy. May Allāh ﷻ exalt the rank and send peace upon the best of mankind, Muḥammad ibn 'Abdullah, and upon his family and his Companions, collectively. As to what follows:

Questions Relating to the Jinn, Magic & Conjuring

The Angels and Jinn

QUESTION: During our current time, there is a lot of conversation amongst the people concerning the *jinn* possessing and entering humans. Some people reject this; rather, some of them reject the existence of the *jinn* completely. Does this affect the belief of the Muslim? Are there any narrations that necessitate belief in the *jinn*? What is the difference between the *jinn* and the angels?

ANSWER: Denying the existence of the *jinn* is disbelief and apostasy from Islām because this is denial of what appears in numerous places in the Qur'ān and the Sunnah, which informs us of their existence.

Belief in the existence of the *jinn* is from belief in the unseen because we do not see them.

Our belief in their existence is based upon the reports from the Most Truthful. Allāh, the Exalted, said about Iblīs and his troops:

﴿ إِنَّهُ يَرَاكُمْ هُوَ وَقَبِيلُهُ مِنْ حَيْثُ لَا تَرَوْنَهُمْ ﴿٢٧﴾ ﴾

Indeed, he sees you, he and his tribe, from where you do not see them.[1]

As for denying *jinn* possession, this does not necessitate disbelief; although denying *jinn* possession is incorrect, and to deny this is to belie what has been affirmed by the legislative proofs and evidences and the recurrent reality that exists. But because this affair is invisible, those who oppose it are not deemed as disbelievers. Denying *jinn* possession is an error, and their denial is not based upon proofs and evidences. Rather, they only base their denial upon their intellect and what they can perceive. The intellect is not used as a benchmark as it relates to matters of the unseen. And the intellect is not given precedence over the legislative evidences, except by the people of misguidance.

The angels and *jinn* differ in a number of ways. The first way is in the origin of their creation. The *jinn* were created from smokeless fire, while the angels were created from light.

---

[1] Sūrah al-'Aʿrāf, 7:27

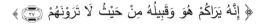

The second way they differ is that the angels are slaves who are always obedient to Allāh ﷻ. They are close to Allāh and honorable. As Allāh, the Exalted, said:

﴿ بَلْ عِبَادٌ مُّكْرَمُونَ ﴿٢٦﴾ لَا يَسْبِقُونَهُ بِالْقَوْلِ وَهُم بِأَمْرِهِ يَعْمَلُونَ ﴿٢٧﴾ ﴾

Rather, they are but honored slaves. They speak not until He has spoken, and they act on His Command.[1]

Allāh, the Exalted, said:

﴿ لَّا يَعْصُونَ اللَّهَ مَا أَمَرَهُمْ وَيَفْعَلُونَ مَا يُؤْمَرُونَ ﴿٦﴾ ﴾

They do not disobey Allāh in what He commands them, but do what they are commanded.[2]

As for the *jinn*, some of them are believers while some of them are disbelievers. Allāh ﷻ has said concerning them:

﴿ وَأَنَّا مِنَّا الْمُسْلِمُونَ وَمِنَّا الْقَاسِطُونَ ﴿١٤﴾ ﴾

And of us some are Muslims, and of us some are al-Qāsiṭūn (disbelievers, those who have deviated from the Right Path).[3]

[1] Sūrah al-'Anbiyā', 21:26-27

[2] Sūrah at-Taḥrīm, 66:6

[3] Sūrah al-Jinn, 72:14

Some of the *jinn* are obedient, while others are disobedient. Allāh, the Exalted, said:

﴿ وَأَنَّا مِنَّا الصَّالِحُونَ وَمِنَّا دُونَ ذَٰلِكَ ﴾

There are among us some that are righteous, and some the contrary.[1]

Curing Jinn Possession and the Evil Eye by Reciting the Qur'ān

QUESTION: During these days, we hear about some people who remedy those afflicted with epilepsy, *jinn* possession, and the evil eye by reciting the Qur'ān. We find that some people have a satisfactory result when receiving treatment from those who utilize these methods. Is there anything forbidden in the actions of those who use these methods? Are those who go to them sinning? What are the conditions you believe should be present within those who treat the sick by reciting the Qur'ān? Has it been narrated that some of the Salaf treated those afflicted with magic and epilepsy by reciting the Qur'ān?

ANSWER: There is no problem with treating those afflicted with epilepsy, the evil eye and magic by reciting the Qur'ān. This is known as *ruqya*. This is when the reciter recites and blows on the afflicted. Performing *ruqya* with the Qur'ān and supplications is

---

[1] Sūrah al-Jinn, 72:11

permissible. The *ruqya* that is impermissible is that which involves shirk (polytheism). This is that which involves supplicating to other than Allāh ﷻ and seeking help from the *jinn* and devils. These are the actions of charlatans and liars. They call upon unknown names. As for *ruqya* using the Qur'ān and supplications that have been narrated, this is prescribed in Islām.

Allāh ﷻ has made the Qur'ān a healing for physical sickness, such as that of the body; and spiritual sickness, such as that of the heart. The condition is that the reciter and patient must have sincere intentions. Both of them must believe that the healing comes from Allāh ﷻ and that the *ruqya*, using the Speech of Allāh, is a means from the beneficial means.

There is no harm in going to them for treatment using the Qur'ān if they are known for being upright. Meaning, they have sound *'aqīdah*, do not use *ruqya* that contains polytheism, do not utilize the *jinn* or devils, and they only use the legislative *ruqya*.

Using the Qur'ān as *ruqya* is from the Sunnah of the Messenger of Allāh ﷺ and from the action of the Salaf ﵏. They would use the Qur'ān to treat those afflicted with the evil eye, epilepsy, magic and all illnesses. They believed this was a beneficial means to cure the sick, while believing that Allāh ﷻ alone is the One who heals.

We must warn you that some charlatans and liars may mention something from the Qur'ān or supplications, but they blend it with polytheism and seeking help from the *jinn* and devils. Some ignorant people hear them and believe they are using the Qur'ān to treat the sick. This deception must be warned against.

Books About the Jinn

QUESTION: The questioner asks about the book *'Ākam al-Murjān Concerning the Oddities and Rulings of the Jinn.*

ANSWER: *'Ākam al-Murjān Concerning the Oddities and Rulings of the Jinn*[1], this book is known. It is research into the affairs of the *jinn* from the standpoint of the rulings concerning them, their appearance and their actions. It brings broad insight concerning them. It has benefit for the reader, and it contains legislative rulings. It is a good book in general.

The Cure and Protection from Envy

QUESTION: What is the cure for envy, and what is the prescribed method to protection oneself from it?

---

[1] Translator's note: This book was written by Muḥammad ibn 'Abdullah ash-Shibli, who died 769 years after the migration.

ANSWER: Envy is a dangerous disease and severely damaging. Envy is when someone desires the removal of Allāh's favor from those He has bestowed it upon. Envy is in opposition to Allāh ﷻ, and it is from the attributes of the Jews and disbelievers. Allāh, the Exalted, said:

﴿ مَّا يَوَدُّ الَّذِينَ كَفَرُوا مِنْ أَهْلِ الْكِتَابِ وَلَا الْمُشْرِكِينَ أَن يُنَزَّلَ عَلَيْكُم مِّنْ خَيْرٍ مِّن رَّبِّكُمْ ﴿١٠٥﴾ ﴾

Neither those who disbelieve from the People of the Scripture, nor the polytheists, wish that any good should be sent down to you from your Lord.[1]

And Allāh, the Exalted, said:

﴿ وَدَّ كَثِيرٌ مِّنْ أَهْلِ الْكِتَابِ لَوْ يَرُدُّونَكُم مِّن بَعْدِ إِيمَانِكُمْ كُفَّارًا حَسَدًا مِّنْ عِندِ أَنفُسِهِم مِّن بَعْدِ مَا تَبَيَّنَ لَهُمُ الْحَقُّ ﴿١٠٩﴾ ﴾

Many of the People of the Scripture wish they could turn you back to disbelief after you have believed,

out of envy from themselves [even] after the truth has become clear to them.[2]

[1] Sūrah al-Baqarah, 2:105
[2] Sūrah al-Baqarah, 2:109

Allāh ﷻ said about the Jews who had envy toward Muḥammad:

﴿ أَمْ يَحْسُدُونَ النَّاسَ عَلَىٰ مَا آتَاهُمُ اللَّهُ مِن فَضْلِهِ ﴿٥٤﴾ ﴾

Or do they envy people for what Allāh has given them of His Bounty?[1]

The treatment for the envious person, in order for envy to leave them, is that they must seek refuge with Allāh ﷻ from it and ask Him to cure them. They must remember Allāh and mention Him a lot when they see things that amaze them.

As for the cure for the envied person, he must seek refuge with Allāh ﷻ from the evil of the envious. He should recite Sūrah al-Falaq and Sūrah an-Nās, supplicate to Allāh and place his trust in Him.

Receiving Payment for Ruqya

QUESTION: Is there anything in the pure legislation that prevents treating the sick person by reciting the Noble Qur'ān? Is it permissible for the person performing *ruqya* to take payment or a gift for his work?

ANSWER: As for treating the sick person by reciting the Noble Qur'ān, it is permissible if it is done according to the prescribed method, which is to recite the Qur'ān, blow lightly upon the sick

[1] Sūrah an-Nisā', 4:54

individual or injured area, or into water which the sick person will drink. The Prophet ﷺ received *ruqya*, and he perform it upon others. He allowed it and ordered us to use it.

Al-Suyūṭī said, "The scholars have agreed that *ruqya* is permissible when three conditions are met.

1. That it is performed using the Words of Allāh ﷻ or His Names and Attributes.
2. That it is performed in the Arabic language with words that have clear, known meanings.
3. The person must believe the *ruqya* in and of itself does not have any affect; rather, it is by the decree of Allāh, the Exalted."[1]

Shaykh al-Islām Muḥammad ibn 'Abdul-Wahab said, "Ruqya is what is known as incantations, specifically that which is proven by the evidence and is free from polytheism. The Messenger of Allāh ﷺ has allowed this for the evil eye and fever."[2]

This fever refers to the poisonous scorpion if it stings the person, and the bite of a snake. Surely, *ruqya* will bring about benefit in treating this, by the permission of Allāh ﷻ.

---

[1] Fatḥul Majīd, 1/243

[2] *The Book of Tawḥīd* by Muḥammad ibn 'Abdul-Wahab, 62-63

There is no harm if the person performing *ruqya* takes payment or a gift for his services. This is because the Messenger of Allāh ﷺ agreed with the actions of the Companions who accepted payment for performing *ruqya* upon the man who was stung by the scorpion. He ﷺ said:

إِنَّ أَحَقَّ مَا أَخَذْتُمْ عَلَيْهِ أَجْرًا كِتَابُ اللَّهِ

The most deserving thing by which a wage can be accepted is the Book of Allāh.[1]

Dissolving Qur'ānic Verses in Water to Drink

QUESTION: I write verses from the Qur'ān with dissolvable ink for the patient to drink.[2] Is it permissible for me to write verses from the Noble Qur'ān for the sick person to drink?

ANSWER: It has been narrated that the Messenger of Allāh ﷺ performed *ruqya* upon the sick by directly reciting on them and lightly blowing on their body. This is the *ruqya* that has been narrated from the Prophet ﷺ.[3]

---

[1] Al-Būkharī, 5405

[2] Translator's note: This is when the person writes Qur'ānic verses on paper using saffron—or another dissolvable, edible material—and places the paper in water until the words dissolve.

[3] Refer to al-Būkharī, 7/22, 24, 25, from the *ḥadīth* of 'Ā'isha, may Allah ﷻ be pleased with her.

Likewise, he seeks refuge on behalf of the sick with the words the Prophet ﷺ used to seek refuge. He says:

أُعِيذُك بِكَلِمَاتِ اللهِ التَّامَّاتِ مِنْ شَرِّ مَا خَلَقَ

I seek refuge for you with the perfect Words of Allāh, from the evil which He created.

بِسْمِ اللَّهِ أَرْقِيكَ، مِنْ كُلِّ شَيْءٍ يُؤْذِيكَ، مِنْ شَرِّ كُلِّ نَفْسٍ أَوْ عَيْنِ حَاسِدٍ، اللَّهُ يَشْفِيكَ

In the Name of Allāh I perform ruqya upon you from everything that harms you, and from every evil soul or envious eye; may Allāh heal you.

رَبّنَا اللّهُ الذِي فِي السَّمَاءِ، تَقَدَّسَ اسمُكَ، أَمرُكَ فِي السَّمَاءِ وَالأَرْضِ، كَمَا رَحمَتُكَ فِي السَّمَاءِ فَاجْعَلْ رَحْمَتَكَ فِي الأَرْضِ، اغفِر لَنَا حَوْبَنَا وَخَطَايَانَا، أَنتَ رَبُّ الطَّيِّبِينَ، أَنزِلْ رَحْمَةً مِن رَحمَتِكَ، وَشِفَاءً مِن شِفَائِكَ

Our Lord is Allāh, the One who is above the heavens, Holy is Your Name, Your command is implemented in the heavens and the earth. Just as Your mercy is in the heavens, place Your mercy in the earth. Forgive us our misdeeds and our sins. You are the Lord

of the good. Send down a mercy from Your mercy and a healing from Your healing.[1]

There are other supplications as well which are recited over the sick person.

As for writing the Noble Qur'ān on paper, dishes, or utensils, dissolving the words, then the sick person drinking the dissolved words, some scholars have said this is allowable and they include this in *ruqya*. But the *ruqya* we mentioned is more befitting. This is for the person to perform *ruqya* directly on the sick. Either he recites on him, or he recite in some water and the sick person drinks it; as has been narrated from the Prophet peace be upon him. This is more befitting and doing so restricts the person to what is proven by the evidence. And Allāh ﷻ knows best.

QUESTION: What is the Islāmic ruling on writing verses from the Noble Qur'ān or some of the Names of Allāh ﷻ and dissolving them in water with the intention of healing or bringing about benefit?

ANSWER: It is best to treat the patient by directly reciting the Qur'ān over the sick individual. Thus, you perform *ruqya* by reciting the Qur'ān and lightly blowing directly over the sick person. This is more beneficial, better, and more complete. This is how it was done by the Messenger of Allāh ﷺ. And this is how the Salaf ﵏ performed *ruqya*.

[1] Saḥiḥ al-Būkharī, 7/24-26 and Saḥiḥ Muslim, 4/1718

Likewise, it is permissible to recite in water and pour this water for the sick to drink, because this has been narrated in various *aḥadīth*.

As for writing the Qur'ān on a clean, pure surface, such as a dish or pure paper, and dissolving the written words so the sick can drink it; some of the Salaf like Imām Aḥmad ﵀ permitted this.[1] Ibn Taymiyyah ﵀ mentioned this in his collection of fatāwā[2], as did Ibn al-Qayyim ﵀ in *Zād al-Mā'ād*.[3] This was a practice known amongst some of the Salaf ﵏, but it is better to avoid it and limit yourself to that which has been narrated. And Allāh ﷻ knows best.

Going to Magicians to Resolve Marital Problems

QUESTION: Before I was guided and started praying regularly, in the proper time, and before I began to recite the Noble Qur'ān, I went to a magician who requested I strangle a chicken. The purpose of this was to make a link between my husband and me, because there were always problems between us. I strangled the chicken with my hands. Is there any sin upon me for this action? What can I do to free myself of this fear and stress which haunts me?

---

[1] Refer to *Affairs and Treatise*, 2/112, 114
[2] Refer to *Collection of Fatawa*, 19/64-65
[3] Refer to *Zād al-Mā'ād*, 4/170-171

ANSWER: Firstly, going to magicians is impermissible, with a severe prohibition, because magic is disbelief and harmful to the slaves of Allāh, the Exalted. Thus, going to magicians is a tremendous crime. Strangling a chicken is another crime because this is punishing an animal, killing it unjustly and seeking nearness to other than Allāh ﷻ with this action is polytheism. But if you repented to Allāh, the Exalted, with a correct repentance, Allāh will forgive your previous action. Do not return to this in the future. Allāh ﷻ forgives those who repent to Him.

It is not permissible for the Muslims to allow the magicians to spread their magic amongst the Muslims. Rather, they must disapprove of this; and the leaders of the Muslim governments must execute the magicians in order to relieve the Muslims of their evil.

Utilizing Amulets to Cure the Sick

QUESTION: We live on the mountain. When one of our children or animals becomes sick we go to the Shaykh and he writes some words on a piece of paper. We burn or vaporize this paper and drink the remnants, or we tie the words around the neck of the sick person or animal. What is the ruling of this action, may Allāh bless you?

ANSWER: We do not know what is written on this piece of paper. Perhaps he wrote words of disbelief or words that associate partners with Allāh ﷻ, which come from these charlatans. At any rate it is incumbent to stay away from this, and you must place you trust and reliance in Allāh, the Exalted.

Allāh ﷻ said:

﴿ وَإِن يَمْسَسْكَ اللَّهُ بِضُرٍّ فَلَا كَاشِفَ لَهُ إِلَّا هُوَ وَإِن يُرِدْكَ بِخَيْرٍ فَلَا رَادَّ لِفَضْلِهِ ﴿١٠٧﴾ ﴾

And if Allāh touches you with hurt, there is none who can remove it but He; and if He intends any good for you, there is none who can repel His favor.[1]

And Allāh, the Exalted, said:

﴿ وَإِن يَمْسَسْكَ اللَّهُ بِضُرٍّ فَلَا كَاشِفَ لَهُ إِلَّا هُوَ وَإِن يَمْسَسْكَ بِخَيْرٍ فَهُوَ عَلَىٰ كُلِّ شَيْءٍ قَدِيرٌ ﴿١٧﴾ ﴾

And if Allāh touches you with harm, none can remove it but He, and if He touches you with good, then He is Able to do all things.[2]

'Ibrāhīm ﷺ said:

﴿ وَإِذَا مَرِضْتُ فَهُوَ يَشْفِينِ ﴿٨٠﴾ ﴾

---

[1] Sūrah Yūnus, 10:107
[2] Sūrah al-'An'ām, 6:17

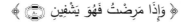

And when I am ill, it is He who cures me.[1]

Thus, when seeking a cure, it is incumbent upon the Muslim to place his trust in Allāh ﷻ by supplication to Him, worshipping Him, and humbling himself to Allāh alone. Allāh is the One who controls the cure and healing.

As for going to the Shaykh—as the questioner called him—taking papers from them, burning the paper and inhaling the remnants or the like, this action must be abandoned. Likewise, it is not permissible to hang these words around the necks of animals because this is the hanging of amulets. The Prophet ﷺ forbade us from hanging amulets, and he deemed it to be polytheism.[2]

Use the medicine which Allāh ﷻ has permitted. Allāh did not send down any disease except that He sent down a cure for it. Those who know it know it, and those who are ignorant of it are ignorant of it. Therefore, it is upon you to take the permissible medicine.

Working in a Church

QUESTION: I took a job in a church for a daily salary. What is the ruling on the money I took, is it permissible or impermissible?

[1] Sūrah ash-Shu'arā', 26:80

[2] Collected by Aḥmad, 4/154-156

ANSWER: It is not permissible for the Muslims to work in places of *shirk* (polytheism) and where other than Allāh ﷻ is worshipped, such as churches, shrines and the like. To do so is to affirm their falsehood and assist them upon it. This work is impermissible. It is not permissible for the Muslim to take this job, and the wage he earned doing this job is an impermissible wage. It is upon you to repent to Allāh, the Exalted. If you give the money you earned from this job in charity it will be more complete in absolving you of the sin, and proof of the correctness of your regret and repentance.

In summary, it is not permissible for the Muslim to assist the people of falsehood. He cannot work in the places of *shirk* and where idols are present, such as churches, shrines and other than that from the actions of the disbelievers and pagans. This is because it helps them in their falsehood and affirms their evil. Therefore, the salary earned from this is impermissible. And with Allāh ﷻ refuge is sought.

Going to a Shaykh for Reentry into Islām

QUESTION: I am a married man. There was a misunderstanding between my wife and I, so I beat her severely. Due to her anger she tore the garment that she was wearing. I heard that whoever tears their garment exits from the fold of Islām, and it becomes obligatory upon them to go to the "Shaykh," so he can recite some verses from the Qur'ān and some *ḥadīth* over them. The person will recite after him, and by doing so the "Shaykh" will reenter the person into the fold of Islām. Is this correct? And is there a sin upon me for severely beating my wife?

ANSWER: Firstly, you made a mistake in the manner in which you dealt with your wife by beating her. It is not permissible for a man to beat his wife. He can only discipline her in accordance with the legislation, within the limits of the legislation. If the wife is disobedient and refuses to listen to her husband, Allāh, the Exalted, said:

﴿ وَاللَّاتِي تَخَافُونَ نُشُوزَهُنَّ فَعِظُوهُنَّ وَاهْجُرُوهُنَّ فِي الْمَضَاجِعِ
وَاضْرِبُوهُنَّ ۖ فَإِنْ أَطَعْنَكُمْ فَلَا تَبْغُوا عَلَيْهِنَّ سَبِيلًا ﴿٣٤﴾ ﴾

As to those women on whose part you see ill-conduct, admonish them (first), (next) refuse to share their beds, (and last) beat them (lightly, if it is useful), but if they return to obedience, seek not against them means (of annoyance).[1]

As for your wife tearing her garment, this was an error on her part because it is not permissible for the Muslim to tear their garment due to discontentment. This is an action from the pre-Islāmic days of ignorance. It is obligatory upon the Muslim to remain patient and seek the reward from Allāh ﷻ. Therefore, what this woman did was not permissible because it is based on discontent, but it does not remove her

[1] Sūrah an-Nisā', 4:34

from the fold of Islām. It does not take the person outside of Islām, but this action is not permissible.

As for going to a "Shaykh" so he can do such and such, this is a major mistake, and this is not from the religion of Islām. When the person sins, he repents to Allāh ﷻ; and he does not go to see a "Shaykh." This is the action of the Christian. The Christians go to see their priests and monks to free themselves from sins, as they allege. As for the Muslim, then Allāh ﷻ has command them with repentance which is between them and Allāh. Allāh accepts the repentance of the one who repents, and thus the person has no need to go to a "Shaykh."

Clinics for Those Possessed

QUESTION: What is your view on opening clinics specifically for reciting upon those afflicted?

ANSWER: It is not permissible to do this because this opens a door to *fitnah* (trouble and difficulty). This opens the door for scam artists. This was not from the actions of the Salaf ﷺ. They did not open clinics or centers to recite upon those afflicted.

Going to great lengths in this matter brings about evil. The evil people will enter, and those who are not qualified will become involved. The people will follow their desires and want to draw the people to them, even if they have to do prohibited acts in order to attract them. It should not be said, "This is okay because the man in charge is righteous." Because the people will be put to trial and tested by way of this. Thus, even if the person is righteous, opening the door to this affair is not permissible.

Is It Permissible to See A Psychiatrist?

QUESTION: My wife suffers from various illnesses. I took her to see some doctors and they said they did not find any physical illness present within her. Thus, she suspects she may be afflicted with magic. She often asks me to take her to individuals who remove magic, but I refuse to do so due to the prohibition of this. At this point I do not have a comfortable marital life with her. What do you see as the solution?

ANSWER: Every illness which afflicts the person is not magic. There are many illnesses, so every sickness is not magic. This is from the standpoint of suspicion. It is obligatory to abandon suspicion and whispers, and the person must seek shelter with Allāh ﷻ by supplicating to Him. Performing *ruqya* is permissible according to the legislation of Islām. This is done by reciting the Qur'ān upon the sick person. This should be repeated numerous times. Likewise, refuge should be sought with Allāh ﷻ by reciting the various supplications for seeking refuge. There is no harm in going to see a psychiatrist. Perhaps they know what type of illness she is suffering from, and they may have with them a treatment for this.

If it is confirmed that it is indeed magic, then magic is not treated with magic. It is only treated by way of the legislated treatment, which is to recite the Qur'ān. If there are some permissible medicines which are known to remove magic, then this can be utilized also.

Do not go to a magician to remove magic, this is not permissible. Hasan al-Basrī said, "No one removes magic by using magic except for a magician." The Messenger of Allāh ﷺ was asked about a charm for one who is possessed. He ﷺ said:

هُوَ مِنْ عَمَلِ الشَّيْطَانِ

This is from the works of Shayṭān.[1]

These charms, known as *nashrah*, remove magic by using magic similar to it.

Can a Woman Go to a Male Shaykh For Ruqya?

QUESTION: Is it permissible for a woman afflicted with magic to go to a Shaykh so he may recite over her?

ANSWER: There is no problem with this if the Shaykh is known for piety; religiosity; sound, correct *'aqīdah* (Islāmic creed and belief); he recites the Qur'ān over her while she is concealed from him and properly covered; he is not secluded with her; and he is safe from

---

[1] Sunan Abi Dāwūd, 3868

fitnah. This is because if all the above conditions are met, then that which prohibits this will not exist.

But if this individual is not known to have sound, correct *'aqīdah,* no one should go to him. Likewise, if he takes lightly the matter of being around women, she should not go to him. If he touches or looks at women, she should not go to him due to the presence of temptation and tribulation.

How to Undo Magic If You Cannot Locate It?

QUESTION: There is a family complaining of a significant increase in problems and differing amongst them. There was some friction between them and some foreign nationals who practice magic. The reason for the mistrust is because they found fingernails and hair in some of the maids' purses. Their question is how can they treat these problems if they do not know where the magic is located?

ANSWER: They should take what they found (fingernails and hair) and destroy it. And they should take those maids who practice magic to the embassy and have them deported from the country. They should not allow them to continue working for them or anyone else.

Wearing Amulets to Protect Against Magic

QUESTION: What is the ruling on wearing amulets? Is the person who uses amulets considered a soothsayer?

ANSWER: If the amulets have words in other than the Arabic language, or unconnected letters, then it is not permissible to use them according to the consensus of the scholars. If the amulets contain words written from the Qur'ān, *ḥadīth* or legislated supplications, then the scholars differ about its permissibility. The most correct viewpoint is that this is likewise impermissible. This is because the Prophet ﷺ prohibited wearing talismans. And a talisman is anything hung to seek protection, whether it contains the Qur'ān or not.

Placing the Muṣḥaf Beside the Unattended Child to Protect from the Jinn

QUESTION: What is your view on the mother who places the *muṣḥaf* beside her young child in order to protect him from the *jinn* during times she is busy and unable to attend to him?

ANSWER: This is not permissible because it is belittlement of the *muṣḥaf*, and likewise because this action has not been legislated.

Magicians and Fortunetellers

Are There Permissible Types of Magic?

QUESTION: We would like for you to explain the reality of magic. Are there any types of permissible magic? Does practicing magic remove the magician from the fold of Islām?

ANSWER: The linguistic meaning of magic is: an imperceptible action, the reason for which is hidden. The reality of magic was explained by al-Muwaffaq[1] in *al-Kaafi.* He said, "Magic is a term used for charms, spells, and knots, that affects the heart and body. Magic can make people sick, kill them, and cause separation between husband and wife."[2]

All magic is impermissible, and there is no type of permissible magic. Allāh, the Exalted, said:

﴿ وَلَقَدْ عَلِمُوا لَمَنِ اشْتَرَاهُ مَا لَهُ فِي الْآخِرَةِ مِنْ خَلَاقٍ ﴿١٠٢﴾ ﴾

---

[1] Muwaffaq al-Dīn Abū Muḥammad, commonly known as ibn Qudāmah

[2] *Al-Kāfī Concerning the Fiqh of Imam Ahmad,* 4/164

And indeed, they knew that the buyers of it (magic) would have no share in the Hereafter.[1]

This means the practitioner of magic will have no portion in the Hereafter. Hasan said, "There is no religion for the practitioner of magic."[2]

This verse proves the prohibition of magic, and it proves the disbelief of the user. The Prophet ﷺ listed magic as being from the seven deadly destructive sins. And it is incumbent upon the Muslim ruler to execute the magician. Imām Aḥmad said, "It has been affirmed that three companions of the Prophet ﷺ executed magicians."[3] The three companions who executed magicians were 'Umar ibn al-Khattāb, Ḥafṣa and Jundab, may Allāh ﷻ be pleased with them.

Learning magic, teaching magic, and practicing magic is disbelief in Allāh, the Exalted, which removes the person from the fold of Islām. The magician is executed to relieve the people of his evil if it is affirmed that he is indeed a magician. The magician is a disbeliever and his evil extends throughout the community.

---

[1] Sūrah al-Baqarah, 2:102

[2] Tafsir ibn Kathīr, 1/137

[3] Affairs and treatises narrated from Imām Aḥmad concerning *'aqīdah.*

Do Fortunetellers and Soothsayers Know the Unseen?

QUESTION: Is it correct to say that magicians, soothsayers, fortunetellers, and clairvoyants know many affairs of the unseen? And how can we refute their information when some of what they predict occurs in the future?

ANSWER: They may inform the people of some matters they hear from the devils when the devils eavesdrop, or some matters which are hidden from humans while seen by the devils. Thus, their workers from the devils and mankind inform the people of what the devils from the *jinn* told them. These affairs are not unseen as it relates to the devils because they hear it or see it; but the devils add one hundred lies to each single statement they hear. Yet the people believe everything they say due to this one true statement they heard from the heavens. Allāh, the Exalted, said:

﴿ هَلْ أُنَبِّئُكُمْ عَلَىٰ مَن تَنَزَّلُ الشَّيَاطِينُ ﴿٢٢١﴾ تَنَزَّلُ عَلَىٰ كُلِّ أَفَّاكٍ أَثِيمٍ
﴿٢٢٢﴾ يُلْقُونَ السَّمْعَ وَأَكْثَرُهُمْ كَاذِبُونَ ﴿٢٢٣﴾ ﴾

Shall I inform you upon whom the devils descend? They descend upon every sinful liar. Who gives ear (to the devils), and most of them are liars.[1]

[1] Sūrah ash-Shu'arā', 26:221-223

As for knowledge of the unseen, then it only belongs to Allāh ﷻ specifically. No one knows it except for Him. Allāh, the Exalted, said:

﴿ قُل لَّا يَعْلَمُ مَن فِي السَّمَاوَاتِ وَالْأَرْضِ الْغَيْبَ إِلَّا اللَّهُ ﴿٦٥﴾ ﴾

Say: None in the heavens and the earth knows the unseen except Allāh.[1]

And He ﷻ said:

﴿ وَعِندَهُ مَفَاتِحُ الْغَيْبِ لَا يَعْلَمُهَا إِلَّا هُوَ ﴿٥٩﴾ ﴾

And with Him are the keys of the unseen, none knows them but He.[2]

Asking Magicians for Assistance If No One is Harmed

QUESTION: Is it permissible to ask magicians for help to take care of some needs if their assistance does not involve harming others?

ANSWER: Magic is impermissible and disbelief. It is likewise impermissible to teach it or learn it. Allāh, the Exalted, said:

---

[1] Sūrah an-Naml, 27:65

[2] Sūrah al-'An'ām, 6:59

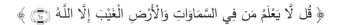

﴿ وَاتَّبَعُوا مَا تَتْلُو الشَّيَاطِينُ عَلَىٰ مُلْكِ سُلَيْمَانَ ۖ وَمَا كَفَرَ سُلَيْمَانُ وَلَٰكِنَّ
الشَّيَاطِينَ كَفَرُوا يُعَلِّمُونَ النَّاسَ السِّحْرَ وَمَا أُنزِلَ عَلَى الْمَلَكَيْنِ بِبَابِلَ هَارُوتَ
وَمَارُوتَ ۚ وَمَا يُعَلِّمَانِ مِنْ أَحَدٍ حَتَّىٰ يَقُولَا إِنَّمَا نَحْنُ فِتْنَةٌ فَلَا تَكْفُرْ ۖ
فَيَتَعَلَّمُونَ مِنْهُمَا مَا يُفَرِّقُونَ بِهِ بَيْنَ الْمَرْءِ وَزَوْجِهِ ۚ وَمَا هُم بِضَارِّينَ بِهِ مِنْ
أَحَدٍ إِلَّا بِإِذْنِ اللَّهِ ۚ وَيَتَعَلَّمُونَ مَا يَضُرُّهُمْ وَلَا يَنفَعُهُمْ ۚ وَلَقَدْ عَلِمُوا لَمَنِ اشْتَرَاهُ
مَا لَهُ فِي الْآخِرَةِ مِنْ خَلَاقٍ ۚ وَلَبِئْسَ مَا شَرَوْا بِهِ أَنفُسَهُمْ ۚ لَوْ
كَانُوا يَعْلَمُونَ ﴿١٠٢﴾ ﴾

They followed what the devils gave out (falsely of the magic) in the lifetime of Sulayman. Sulayman did not disbelieve, but the devils disbelieved, teaching men magic and such things that came down at Babylon to the two angels, Harut and Marut, but neither of these two (angels) taught anyone (such things) till they had said, "We are only for trial, so disbelieve not (by learning this magic from us)." And from these (angels) people learn that by which they cause separation between man and his wife, but they could not thus harm anyone except by Allāh's Leave. And they learn that which harms them and profits them not. And indeed, they knew that the buyers of it (magic) would have no share in the Hereafter. And how bad indeed

was that for which they sold their ownselves, if they but knew.[1]

It is not permissible to use magic to take care of some needs because magic is impermissible and disbelief. It is not permissible for a Muslim to use anything which is *ḥarām* and disbelief; rather, it must be disapproved of. The magicians must be executed by the Muslim rulers in order to save the Muslims from their evil.

Was Magic Placed Upon the Prophet Peace Be Upon Him?

QUESTION: Is it true that magic was placed upon the Prophet ﷺ? If it is true, how did the magic affect him? How did he deal with the individual who put magic on him?

ANSWER: Yes, it is true that magic was placed on the Prophet ﷺ. 'Ā'isha, may Allāh be pleased with her, said:

سُحِرَ النَّبِيُّ صلى الله عليه وسلم حَتَّى إِنَّهُ لَيُخَيَّلُ إِلَيْهِ أَنَّهُ يَفْعَلُ الشَّىْءَ
وَمَا فَعَلَهُ، حَتَّى إِذَا كَانَ ذَاتَ يَوْمٍ وَهْوَ عِنْدِي دَعَا اللَّهَ وَدَعَاهُ، ثُمَّ قَالَ
أَشَعَرْتِ يَا عَائِشَةُ أَنَّ اللَّهَ قَدْ أَفْتَانِي فِيمَا اسْتَفْتَيْتُهُ فِيهِ ". قُلْتُ وَمَا ذَاكَ يَا
رَسُولَ اللَّهِ قَالَ " جَاءَنِي رَجُلاَنِ، فَجَلَسَ أَحَدُهُمَا عِنْدَ رَأْسِي وَالآخَرُ عِنْدَ

[1] Sūrah al-Baqarah, 2:102

رِجْلَيَّ، ثُمَّ قَالَ أَحَدُهُمَا لِصَاحِبِهِ مَا وَجَعُ الرَّجُلِ قَالَ مَطْبُوبٌ. قَالَ وَمَنْ طَبَّهُ قَالَ لَبِيدُ بْنُ الأَعْصَمِ، الْيَهُودِيُّ مِنْ بَنِي زُرَيْقٍ. قَالَ فِيمَا ذَا قَالَ فِي مُشْطٍ وَمُشَاطَةٍ، وَجُفِّ طَلْعَةٍ ذَكَرٍ. قَالَ فَأَيْنَ هُوَ قَالَ فِي بِئْرِ ذِي أَرْوَانَ

Magic was worked on the Messenger of Allāh peace be upon him so that he began to imagine that he had done something although he had not. One day while he was with me, he invoked Allāh and invoked for a long period and then said, "O 'Ā'isha! Do you know that Allāh has instructed me regarding the matter I asked Him about?" I asked, "What is that, O Messenger of Allāh?" He said, "Two men came to me; one of them sat near my head and the other sat near my feet. One of them asked his companion, 'What is ailing this man?' The other replied, 'He is under the effect of magic.' The first one asked, 'Who has worked magic on him?' The other replied, 'Labid bin A'sam, a Jew from the tribe of Bani Zuraiq.' The (first one asked), 'With what has it been done?' The other replied, 'With a comb and the hair stuck to it and a skin of the pollen of a male date palm tree.' The first one asked, 'Where is it?' The other replied, 'In the well of Dharwan.'"[1]

[1] Saḥiḥ al-Bukhārī 5766

Imām ibn al-Qayyim said, "Some people reject this, and say it is not possible that he was affected by magic. They believe this is a deficiency and defect, but the affair is not as they allege. Rather, this is similar to the other illnesses that affected the Prophet ﷺ, such as sickness and hunger. It is an illness from among the many diseases. He was afflicted by it just as he was poisoned, and there is no difference between the two."[1]

Al-Qāḍī ibn 'Iyāḍ may Allāh have mercy upon him said, "This does not diminish his status as a prophet. As for him believing he ﷺ had done something that he had not done, this does not affect his truthfulness due to the proof and consensus that he was infallible in the religion. This is from the affairs that can happen to him in the worldly life, because this is not the purpose for which he ﷺ was sent or the reason for his virtue. He was exposed to harm like all men. The magic caused him to believe he had done things he had not done, and then he was cured and returned to normal."[2]

When the Prophet ﷺ became aware that magic had been placed upon him, he supplicated to Allāh ﷻ and Allāh directed him to the location of the magic. He ﷺ removed the magic from its place, untied it and he was cured. It was as though he was released from shackles.

---

[1] Zād al-Mā'ād, 4/124

[2] Zād al-Mā'ād, 4/124

The Prophet ﷺ did not punish the Jew who placed magic upon him. The people said to the Prophet ﷺ, “Shall we not seize this wicked man and kill him?” The Prophet ﷺ responded:

لاَ أَمَّا أَنَا فَقَدْ شَفَانِي اللَّهُ، وَأَكْرَهُ أَنْ أُثِيرَ عَلَى أَحَدٍ مِنَ النَّاسِ شَرًّا

No. As for me, then surely Allāh has cured me. And I hate to spread evil among the people.[1]

Protection from Magic

QUESTION: What are the legislative means to protecting oneself from magic? What is the cure for the person afflicted with magic?

ANSWER: The legislative means to cure magic are those that have been mentioned by ibn al-Qayyim. He said, “Two means to remove magic have been narrated from the Prophet ﷺ. One method—and this method is the most effective—is to extract the magic and untie it. This method was mentioned concerning the Messenger of Allāh ﷺ. Zayd bin 'Arqām said:

سَحَرَ النَّبِيَّ صلى الله عليه وسلم رَجُلٌ مِنَ الْيَهُودِ فَاشْتَكَى لِذَلِكَ أَيَّامًا

فَأَتَاهُ جِبْرِيلُ عَلَيْهِ السَّلاَمُ فَقَالَ إِنَّ رَجُلاً مِنَ الْيَهُودِ سَحَرَكَ عَقَدَ لَكَ عُقَدًا

[1] Saḥiḥ al-Būkharī, 3268

فِي بِئْرِ كَذَا وَكَذَا فَأَرْسَلَ رَسُولُ اللَّهِ صلى الله عليه وسلم فَاسْتَخْرَجُوهَا

فَجِيءَ بِهَا فَقَامَ رَسُولُ اللَّهِ صلى الله عليه وسلم كَأَنَّمَا نُشِطَ مِنْ عِقَالٍ

"A Jewish man cast a spell on the Prophet peace be upon him, and he fell ill as a result of it, for several days. Then Jibrīl, peace be upon him, came to him and said: 'A Jewish man has put a spell on you. In such and such a well there is a knot that he tied for you.' The Messenger of Allāh peace be upon him sent them to take it out and bring it to him. Then the Messenger of Allāh peace be upon him got up as if he had been released from bonds."[1]

Likewise, from the most effective methods of curing the effects of magic are the divinely revealed supplications. This is by reciting verses from the Qur'ān and supplications.[2]

This is the second method to cure magic. It is done by reciting the legislated supplications and reciting the Qur'ān over the person affected. The reciter reads Sūrah al-Fātiḥah, al-'Ikhlāṣ, al-Falāq, an-Nās and other verses from the Qur'ān. He then blows lightly upon the sick person. The person will be cured by the permission of Allāh ﷻ.

---

[1] Sunan an-Nasa'i, 4080

[2] Zād al-Mā'ād, 4/124-127

The Difference Between Magic, Soothsaying, Astrology, and Fortunetelling

QUESTION: Is there a difference between magic, soothsaying, astrology, and fortunetelling with regard to the meaning? Does the same ruling apply to all of them?

ANSWER: Magic is a term used for charms, spells and knots prepared by the magician with the intention of affecting the people by killing them, making them sick, or separating a man from his wife. Magic is disbelief, an evil action and a wicked sickness within the community. Thus, the magicians must be removed to relieve the Muslims from their evil.

Soothsaying (al-Kihānah) is to claim knowledge of the unseen through utilizing the *jinn*. Shaykh 'Abdur-Raḥmān ibn Ḥasan said in his explanation of the *Book of Tawhīd*, "Most of the false prophecies which occur within this *'Ummah* are from the men who are allies of the *jinn*. They receive information from the *jinn* concerning some matters that will happen throughout the land which are hidden from man. The ignorant person believes this to be a miracle or a sign of nobility. Many people are led astray by this, believing the man who narrates from the *jinn* is an ally of Allāh ﷻ, while in reality they are allies to the devil.[1]

It is not permissible to go to a soothsayer. The Prophet ﷺ said:

مَنْ أَتَى عَرَّافًا فَسَأَلَهُ عَنْ شَيْءٍ لَمْ تُقْبَلْ لَهُ صَلاَةٌ أَرْبَعِينَ لَيْلَةً

Whoever goes to a fortuneteller and asks him about anything, his prayers will not be accepted for forty days.[2]

The Prophet ﷺ said:

مَنْ أَتَى كَاهِنًا فَصَدَّقَهُ بِمَا يَقُولُ فَقَدْ كَفَرَ بِمَا أُنْزِلَ عَلَى مُحَمَّدٍ

Whoever goes to a soothsayer and believes what he says has disbelieved in that which was revealed to Muḥammad.[3]

And he ﷺ said:

مَنْ أَتَى كَاهِنًا، أَوْ عَرَّافًا، فَصَدَّقَهُ بِمَا يَقُولُ، فَقَدْ كَفَرَ بِمَا أُنْزِلَ عَلَى مُحَمَّدٍ

[1] Fatḥul Majīd, page 235
[2] Saḥiḥ Muslim, 2230
[3] Jami' at-Tirmiḏī, 135

Whoever goes to a soothsayer or a fortuneteller and believes what he says has disbelieved in that which was revealed to Muḥammad.[1]

Al-Baghawī said, "The fortuneteller is the one who claims knowledge of future events and directs people to lost property to find where it is located. It is said the fortuneteller is the soothsayer.[2]

Ibn Taymiyyah said, "The fortuneteller is a name for the soothsayer, the astrologer, those who practice divination by drawing lines in the sand, and others who claim knowledge of these matters (the unseen) by using these means.[3]

Astrology is the study of the movement of the stars to deduce what will occur upon the earth. It is from the actions found during the pre-Islāmic days of ignorance. Astrology is major polytheism if the person believes the stars have an effect upon the universe.

Palm Readers

QUESTION: Does the ruling for those who go to fortunetellers apply to those who go to palm readers, cup readers and those who draw lines in the sand?

[1] Aḥmad, 2/429

[2] Explanation of the Sunnah by al-Baghawī, 12/182

[3] Collection of *fatāwā* by Ibn Taymiyyah, 35/173

ANSWER: There is no doubt that these myths and pagan acts are from the handiwork of the devil. All of the aforementioned are gateways to polytheism and acts of polytheism. It is not permissible for the Muslim who believes in Allāh ﷻ and the last day to go to any of them or believe in any of them. The Prophet ﷺ said:

مَنْ أَتَى كَاهِنًا، أَوْ عَرَّافًا، فَصَدَّقَهُ بِمَا يَقُولُ، فَقَدْ كَفَرَ بِمَا أُنْزِلَ عَلَى مُحَمَّدٍ

Whoever goes to a soothsayer or a fortuneteller and believes what he says has disbelieved in that which was revealed to Muḥammad.[1]

Therefore, it is not permissible to go to them, ask them any questions, or believe in them. The Muslim must place his trust in Allāh ﷻ, rely upon Allāh, and attach himself to Allāh the Exalted. The Muslim must be cautious of that which will corrupt his religion and destabilize his beliefs and creed; or cause him to stray away from the correct path.

The Explanation of Two Aḥadīth

QUESTION: What are the proper guidelines concerning two *aḥadīth* narrated from the Prophet ﷺ?

[1] Aḥmad, 2/429

كَذبَ المنجِّمون ولو صدقوا

Astrologers lie, even if it turns out to be true.[1]

And the *ḥadīth*:

كان نبي من الأنبياء يخُطُّ؛ فمن وافق خطَّهُ؛ فذاك

There was a Prophet who drew lines, so if anyone does it as he drew lines, that is correct.[2]

What is the ruling on drawing lines in the sand and astrology? Are there narrations where the Prophet ﷺ prohibits these actions?

ANSWER: As for the matter of astrology, it is major *shirk* if the intent of astrology is utilizing the stars to predict future events; belief that stars have an effect upon the universe, rain descending, sickness and others matters. This is a belief present during the pre-Islāmic days of ignorance. Astrology is impermissible, with a severe prohibition.

As for the *ḥadīth* the questioners asked about, "Astrologers lie, even if they tell the truth," I did not find a basis or a chain of narration for it. As for the meaning of this narration, it is correct. The astrologers invent lies against Allāh, the Exalted, because the stars have no connection with the affairs of the universe. Allāh ﷻ is the only One who

---

[1] This narration was not found in any books of *ḥadīth*
[2] Sunan Abi Dāwūd, 3909

controls the affairs of the universe. He is the One who created the stars and created everything else. Allāh created the stars for three purposes: beautification of the sky, missiles to shoot at the devils, and signs to guide the travelers. This is what is proven by way of the Qur'ān; thus, whoever seeks other than this has erred.

The other matters from the myths and sorcery that people use to claim knowledge of the unseen, predict the future, or heal the sick; all of this is included in the ruling of astrology. Fortunetelling is included in this as well because it is obligatory upon the hearts to attach to Allāh; their Creator and the One who disposes the affairs of the universe, the One who possesses harm, benefit, good and evil. In His Hands is all good and He has power over all things. As for these created beings, they are controlled while they have no control over anything.

﴿ وَمِنْ آيَاتِهِ اللَّيْلُ وَالنَّهَارُ وَالشَّمْسُ وَالْقَمَرُ ۚ لَا تَسْجُدُوا لِلشَّمْسِ وَلَا لِلْقَمَرِ وَاسْجُدُوا لِلَّهِ الَّذِي خَلَقَهُنَّ إِن كُنتُمْ إِيَّاهُ تَعْبُدُونَ ﴿٣٧﴾ ﴾

And from among His Signs are the night and the day, and the sun and the moon. Prostrate not to the sun or to the moon, but prostrate to Allāh Who created them, if you worship Him.[1]

[1] Sūrah Fuṣṣilat, 41:37

﴿ إِنَّ رَبَّكُمُ اللَّهُ الَّذِي خَلَقَ السَّمَاوَاتِ وَالْأَرْضَ فِي سِتَّةِ أَيَّامٍ ثُمَّ اسْتَوَىٰ عَلَى الْعَرْشِ يُغْشِي اللَّيْلَ النَّهَارَ يَطْلُبُهُ حَثِيثًا وَالشَّمْسَ وَالْقَمَرَ وَالنُّجُومَ مُسَخَّرَاتٍ بِأَمْرِهِ ۗ أَلَا لَهُ الْخَلْقُ وَالْأَمْرُ ۗ تَبَارَكَ اللَّهُ رَبُّ الْعَالَمِينَ ﴿٥٤﴾ ﴾

Indeed, your Lord is Allāh, Who created the heavens and the earth in six days, and then He rose over the Throne. He brings the night as a cover over the day, seeking it rapidly, and the sun, the moon, the stars subjected to His Command. Surely, His is the Creation and Commandment. Blessed be Allāh, the Lord of all that exists![1]

All these things are created beings that are controlled. They have benefits which Allāh ﷻ has placed within them. But to attach your heart to them, seek help from them, or to seek to remove harm by way of them, this is major *shirk* and from the belief of the pre-Islāmic days of ignorance.

As for the other narration:

كان نبي من الأنبياء يخُطُّ؛ فمن وافق خطَّهُ؛ فذاك

[1] Sūrah al-'A'rāf, 7:54

There was a Prophet who drew lines, so if anyone does it as he drew lines, that is correct.[1]

This *ḥadīth* is authentic. It has been collected in Ṣaḥīḥ Muslim, Aḥmad and others from the *ḥadīth* of Muʿāwiyah ☙.

The scholars have said this was specific to this Prophet ☙, and this was from his miracles. Thus, no one is able to do what he did because this was a miracle specific to him. Therefore, this negates drawing in the sand having any connection with the affairs of the universe, because this was specifically for this particular prophet. And those affairs specific to the prophets and their miracles are not shared with anyone. Therefore, the meaning of this *ḥadīth* is to negate anyone having the ability to draw lines in the sand as this Prophet ☙ did. Rather, it is only fabrication, because no one has the ability to draw lines like this Prophet drew lines.

Performing Magic Tricks

QUESTION: In some countries the people are gathered to witness some exciting feats such as an individual putting a sword or knife in his stomach without being harmed, and other unbelievable feats which are outside the norm. What is the ruling concerning these feats?

---

[1] Sunan Abi Dāwūd, 3909

ANSWER: These individuals are charlatans and liars. These acts are known as illusionary magic. Allāh ﷻ mentioned this as the type of magic performed by the magicians of Pharaoh in His statement:

﴿ فَإِذَا حِبَالُهُمْ وَعِصِيُّهُمْ يُخَيَّلُ إِلَيْهِ مِن سِحْرِهِمْ أَنَّهَا تَسْعَىٰ ﴿٦٦﴾ ﴾

Then behold, their ropes and their sticks, by their magic, appeared to him as though they moved fast.[1]

And He ﷻ said:

﴿ فَلَمَّا أَلْقَوْا سَحَرُوا أَعْيُنَ النَّاسِ وَاسْتَرْهَبُوهُمْ ﴿١١٦﴾ ﴾

So when they threw, they bewitched the eyes of the people, and struck terror into them.[2]

This is known as illusion. They cause the people to see other than the reality, or they perform subtle tricks which appear to the people as though it is reality while it is lies. It may appear to the people that they are harming themselves, or they appear to kill someone then return him to normal. But, in reality, nothing happened at all. Or it will appear to the people that they enter a fire and are not harmed. But, in reality, they never entered the fire. It is only subtle tricks by which they deceive the people.

---

[1] Sūrah Ṭāhā, 20:66

[2] Sūrah Al-'A'rāf, 7:116

It is not permissible to allow them to practice this falsehood and deceive the Muslims with this deception, because this will affect the common Muslims.

Among the people of Banū 'Umayya there was a man who used to play like this. He would appear to slaughter a person and remove his head, then replace his head just as it was before. The people present were amazed. Then Jundab al-Khair al-'Azdi, may Allāh ﷻ be pleased with him, came and killed the man, and said, "If you are truthful bring yourself back to life."[1]

It is not permissible for the Muslim to attend such events by these liars and charlatans, nor is it permissible for the Muslim to believe in them. Rather, it is obligatory to belie them; and it is obligatory upon the Muslim rulers to prevent them, and to punish those who practice this even if they call it "games" or "arts"! Names do not alter the reality or make the impermissible permissible.

Similar to this are those who pretend to drag cars with their hair or lay beneath car tires as the cars drive over them. All of this is from illusionary magic and deception.

---

[1] Siyar A'lam al-Nubala by Imām adh-Dhahabi, 3/176-177

Imām of Masjid Makes Love Potions

QUESTION: An Imām writes amulets containing love potions and a way for the wife to control her husband, and a means for the spouses to separate. Is this magic?

ANSWER: The individual who writes amulets containing love potions or means for separation of the loved ones, this person is a magician. This is what Allāh ﷻ has mentioned about those who teach magic and practice magic. Allāh, the Exalted, said:

﴿ فَيَتَعَلَّمُونَ مِنْهُمَا مَا يُفَرِّقُونَ بِهِ بَيْنَ الْمَرْءِ وَزَوْجِهِ ۚ وَمَا هُم بِضَارِّينَ بِهِ مِنْ أَحَدٍ إِلَّا بِإِذْنِ اللَّهِ ﴿١٠٢﴾ ﴾

And from these (angels) people learn that by which they cause separation between man and his wife, but they could not thus harm anyone except by Allāh's Leave.[1]

This is called as-*sarf*, the magic which turns the person away from another; *al-Atf*, the magic which makes a person attracted to another.

Magic is disbelief in Allāh ﷻ, and the magician is a disbeliever because Allāh mentioned in His Book that magic is disbelief. Allāh, the Exalted, said:

[1] Sūrah al-Baqarah, 2:102

﴿ وَمَا كَفَرَ سُلَيْمَانُ وَلَٰكِنَّ الشَّيَاطِينَ كَفَرُوا يُعَلِّمُونَ النَّاسَ السِّحْرَ وَمَا
أُنزِلَ عَلَى الْمَلَكَيْنِ بِبَابِلَ هَارُوتَ وَمَارُوتَ ۚ وَمَا يُعَلِّمَانِ مِنْ أَحَدٍ
حَتَّىٰ يَقُولَا إِنَّمَا نَحْنُ فِتْنَةٌ فَلَا تَكْفُرْ ۖ فَيَتَعَلَّمُونَ مِنْهُمَا مَا يُفَرِّقُونَ بِهِ
بَيْنَ الْمَرْءِ وَزَوْجِهِ ۚ وَمَا هُم بِضَارِّينَ بِهِ مِنْ أَحَدٍ إِلَّا بِإِذْنِ اللَّهِ ۚ
وَيَتَعَلَّمُونَ مَا يَضُرُّهُمْ وَلَا يَنفَعُهُمْ ۚ وَلَقَدْ عَلِمُوا لَمَنِ اشْتَرَاهُ مَا لَهُ فِي
الْآخِرَةِ مِنْ خَلَاقٍ ﴿١٠٢﴾ ﴾

Sulaymān did not disbelieve, but the devils disbelieved, teaching men magic and such things that came down at Babylon to the two angels, Hārūt and Mārūt, but neither of these two (angels) taught anyone (such things) till they had said, "We are only for trial, so disbelieve not (by learning this magic from us)." And from these (angels) people learn that by which they cause separation between man and his wife, but they could not thus harm anyone except by Allāh's Leave. And they learn that which harms them and profits them not. And indeed, they knew that the buyers of it (magic) would have no share in the Hereafter.[1]

[1] Sūrah al-Baqarah, 2:102

These noble verses are proof that magic is disbelief and learning magic is disbelief; and the magician is a disbeliever. It appears in *ḥadīth* that the legislative punishment for the magician is execution by the sword. He is executed as an apostate from Islām.

An individual like this is not suitable to be an Imām in the prayer because he is not upon the religion of the Muslims. It is not permissible for a disbeliever to lead the prayer, and it is not correct for the Muslims to prayer behind him.

It is upon the Muslim ruler to grab him by the hand and implement the necessary punishment upon him, so he does not bring harm to the community. This is because if magic spreads throughout the community the community will collapse. Humiliation will enter upon them and they will be controlled by these myths and charlatans. And with Allāh refuge is sought.

Going to the Dervish to Remove Magic

QUESTION: Some people go to the Imāms of the dervish. They say, "they have the ability to remove magic!" Is their statement correct?

ANSWER: It's not permissible to go to magicians or to believe them. If a Muslim is afflicted with magic, he cannot treat it with more magic. If a Muslim is afflicted with magic, he must seek shelter with Allāh ﷻ, seek refuge in Him, utilize the legislated supplications, and utilize the Noble Qur'ān to seek a cure. He seeks the cure from Allāh, the Exalted, by reciting His verses and His perfect words. This is what it is incumbent upon the Muslim to do. Whoever places his trust in Allāh ﷻ; he will be sufficed, and whoever seeks refuge in Allāh will be protected.

As for going to these deviant magicians, charlatans, and liars; this will increase the sickness of the soul and the body. This will give control to the devils from mankind and *jinn* over this person. They will spoil his life and corrupt his *'aqīdah.* There is no refuge for the believer from Allāh ﷻ except by going to Allāh.

It is obligatory upon the Muslim to seek protection with Allāh ﷻ, seek refuge in Him, place his trust in Him; and recite His verses; especially Ayat al-Kursī, Sūrah al-Falāq and Sūrah an-Nās. The Book of Allāh is sufficient as a cure for the Muslims.

The Imāms of the dervish are Imāms of deviance and misguidance. It is not permissible to go to them.

Prophet Sulaymān, the Angels and Magic

QUESTION What is the explanation of the following statement of Allāh, the Exalted?

﴿ وَاتَّبَعُوا مَا تَتْلُو الشَّيَاطِينُ عَلَى مُلْكِ سُلَيْمَانَ ۖ وَمَا كَفَرَ سُلَيْمَانُ وَلَٰكِنَّ
الشَّيَاطِينَ كَفَرُوا يُعَلِّمُونَ النَّاسَ السِّحْرَ وَمَا أُنزِلَ عَلَى الْمَلَكَيْنِ بِبَابِلَ

هَارُوتَ وَمَارُوتَ ۚ وَمَا يُعَلِّمَانِ مِنْ أَحَدٍ حَتَّىٰ يَقُولَا إِنَّمَا نَحْنُ فِتْنَةٌ فَلَا تَكْفُرْ ﴿١٠٢﴾

They followed what the devils gave out (falsely of the magic) in the lifetime of Sulaymān. Sulaymān did not disbelieve, but the devils disbelieved, teaching men magic and such things that came down at Babylon to the two angels, Hārūt and Mārūt, but neither of these two (angels) taught anyone (such things) till they had said, "We are only for trial, so disbelieve not (by learning this magic from us)."[1]

ANSWER: The Jews discarded the Torah that contains the affirmation of the Prophecy of Muḥammad ﷺ. They substituted the Torah for the books of magic that the devils used to teach during the era of Sulaymān, the son of Dawūd ﷺ. They invented lies and fabrications; and wrongfully attributed this magic to Sulaymān, although he was completely free of this because magic is disbelief and misguidance. Sulaymān ﷺ is a Prophet from the Prophets of Allāh. The Prophets would never practice what contains disbelief or misguidance. This is only an action of the devils and disbelievers from the sons of Adam ﷺ. Their intent is to cause corruption, cause separation between husband and wife, divide the families, and sow animosity between families.

[1] Sūrah al-Baqarah, 2:102

The two angels who taught magic in Babylon, Iraq only did so as a test for the people and a trial. The two angels advised the people who wanted to learn from them to avoid doing so because it is disbelief. They told the people they were only teaching as a trial and a test, and they were not affirming it as correct.

In addition to the people being told by the angels not to learn magic, those who learned the magic only learned that which would harm the people. Thus, they embarked upon two errors:

1. They learned magic, which is disbelief and not permissible.
2. They used that which would harm the people.

Then Allāh ﷻ informed us that the affair remains in His Hands. No harm or benefit can occur without His decree and permission. Thus, it is upon the Muslim to place his trust in Allāh ﷻ, and rely upon Him to repel the evil of the magicians and those who cause corruption.

Then Allāh ﷻ informed us that the Jews knew learning magic was disbelief which necessitates that those who practice it will not enter paradise; but despite this, they proceeded to learn it due to their disbelief and obstinacy.

The Magic of the Sufis

QUESTION: What is magic? And how can the Muslim avoid falling into it? And if he falls into it what is the cure?

ANSWER: Magic is from the works of the devil. Magic is a term for satanic incantations, knots, and the like. Magic causes harm to the body of the person affected. It can kill the individual or make them sick. It can affect the heart by causing separation between the spouses and loved ones. All of this can only occur by the decree of Allāh ﷻ. As Allāh the Exalted said:

﴿ وَمَا هُم بِضَارِّينَ بِهِ مِنْ أَحَدٍ إِلَّا بِإِذْنِ اللَّهِ ﴾

But they could not thus harm anyone except by Allāh's Leave.[1]

This means it can only cause harm if Allāh has decreed this. Therefore, this necessitates that the Muslim take refuge in Allāh ﷻ, and seek refuge with Allāh from the evil of the magicians. Allāh has commanded His Prophet ﷺ and His believing slaves to seek refuge with the Lord of the daybreak from those who blow in knots.

Included in magic are the illusions which have no reality. This is called illusionary magic. As Allāh, the Exalted, said:

[1] Sūrah al-Baqarah, 2:102

﴿ سَحَرُوا أَعْيُنَ النَّاسِ ﴿١١٦﴾ ﴾

They bewitched the eyes of the people.[1]

And He said:

﴿ فَإِذَا حِبَالُهُمْ وَعِصِيُّهُمْ يُخَيَّلُ إِلَيْهِ مِن سِحْرِهِمْ أَنَّهَا تَسْعَىٰ ﴿٦٦﴾ ﴾

Then behold, their ropes and their sticks, by their magic, appeared to him as though they moved fast.[2]

This is the type of magic used by the charlatans from the Sufis and circus performers.

What Does It Mean To "Believe in Magic"?

QUESTION: What is the authenticity of the *ḥadīth*:

ثَلاثَةٌ لا يَدْخُلُونَ الْجَنَّةَ : مُدْمِنُ الْخَمْرِ ، وَقَاطِعُ الرَّحِمِ ، وَمُصَدِّقٌ بِالسِّحْرِ

Three will not enter paradise: The person addicted to intoxicants, the person who severs the ties of kinship and the person who believes in magic.[3]

---

[1] Sūrah Al-'A'rāf, 7:116

[2] Sūrah Ṭāhā, 20:66

[3] Collected by Aḥmad, 4/399

What constitutes "believing" in magic? Is it to believe the magician has power? Or is it to believe in what the person afflicted with magic sees after being afflicted with magic?

ANSWER: As for the *ḥadīth* the questioner mentioned, "Three will not enter paradise: The person addicted to intoxicants, the person who severs the ties of kinship and the person who believes in magic." This *ḥadīth* has been collected by Imām Aḥmad, ibn Ḥibbān, al-Hakim, and affirmed by adh-Dhahabi, may Allāh ﷻ have mercy upon them all. As for the meaning, this is a severe unrestricted warning for those who believe in magic. Included in this warning is astrology. The Prophet ﷺ said:

مَنِ اقْتَبَسَ عِلْمًا مِنَ النُّجُومِ اقْتَبَسَ شُعْبَةً مِنَ السِّحْرِ زَادَ مَا زَادَ

Whoever learns a branch of astrology, he learns a branch of magic; the more he learns (of the former) the more he learns (of the latter).[1]

Believing in magic is a great sin and major crime because it is obligatory to disbelieve in magicians and astrologers. Those who practice this evil must be apprehended because they mislead the creation with this evil and corrupt their *'aqīdah*. It is proven by the Book and the Sunnah that magic is disbelief and the magician must be executed. To

[1] Sunan Ibn Majah, 3726

believe in magic means agreeing with magic and to affirm the evil way the magicians are upon. It is obligatory to disbelieve in them and warn against them.

As for the effects of magic and what occurs as a result of it, this is something that really occurs and has an effect, such as killing, sickness, separation between spouses, and destroying relationships between people.

As for believing the magician and astrologer concerning the affairs of the unseen, there is a severe warning against this, and this is a major sin. The Messenger of Allāh ﷺ said:

مَنْ أَتَى كَاهِنًا فَصَدَّقَهُ بِمَا يَقُولُ فَقَدْ كَفَرَ بِمَا أُنْزِلَ عَلَى مُحَمَّدٍ

Whoever goes to a soothsayer and believes what he says has disbelieved in that which was revealed to Muḥammad.[1]

Praying Behind a Magician

QUESTION: Is it permissible to pray behind a magician? Is it permissible to believe in magic? Is it permissible to treat magic with other magic if another means is not found?

[1] Jami' at-Tirmidhī, 135

ANSWER: Magic is from the major sins, as the Prophet ﷺ said:

اجْتَنِبُوا السَّبْعَ الْمُوبِقَاتِ " . قِيلَ يَا رَسُولَ اللَّهِ وَمَا هُنَّ قَالَ " الشِّرْكُ بِاللَّهِ وَالسِّحْرُ وَقَتْلُ النَّفْسِ الَّتِي حَرَّمَ اللَّهُ إِلاَّ بِالْحَقِّ وَأَكْلُ مَالِ الْيَتِيمِ وَأَكْلُ الرِّبَا وَالتَّوَلِّي يَوْمَ الزَّحْفِ وَقَذْفُ الْمُحْصَنَاتِ الْغَافِلاَتِ الْمُؤْمِنَاتِ

"Avoid the seven destructive sins." We said, 'What are they, O Messenger of Allāh?' He said, "Associating others with Allāh (shirk); witchcraft; killing a soul whom Allāh has forbidden us to kill, except in cases dictated by Islāmic law; consuming orphans' wealth; consuming usury; fleeing from the battlefield; and slandering chaste, innocent women.[1]

He counted magic from the destructive sins, and he mentioned it after associating partners with Allāh ﷻ. Allāh mentioned that the Jews exchanged the Book of Allāh for magic. Allāh, the Exalted, said:

﴿ وَلَمَّا جَاءَهُمْ رَسُولٌ مِّنْ عِندِ اللَّهِ مُصَدِّقٌ لِّمَا مَعَهُمْ نَبَذَ فَرِيقٌ مِّنَ الَّذِينَ أُوتُوا الْكِتَابَ كِتَابَ اللَّهِ وَرَاءَ ظُهُورِهِمْ كَأَنَّهُمْ لَا يَعْلَمُونَ ﴿١٠١﴾ وَاتَّبَعُوا مَا تَتْلُو الشَّيَاطِينُ عَلَىٰ مُلْكِ سُلَيْمَانَ ۖ وَمَا كَفَرَ سُلَيْمَانُ وَلَٰكِنَّ الشَّيَاطِينَ كَفَرُوا يُعَلِّمُونَ النَّاسَ السِّحْرَ ﴿١٠٢﴾ ﴾

[1] Al-Bukhārī, 3/195

And when there came to them a Messenger from Allāh confirming what was with them, a party of those who were given the Scripture threw away the Book of Allāh behind their backs as if they did not know! They followed what the devils gave out (falsely of the magic) in the lifetime of Sulaymān. Sulaymān did not disbelieve, but the devils disbelieved, teaching men magic.[1]

Magic is from the actions of the devils, and it is disbelief. Allāh ﷻ said:

﴿ وَمَا يُعَلِّمَانِ مِنْ أَحَدٍ حَتَّىٰ يَقُولَا إِنَّمَا نَحْنُ فِتْنَةٌ فَلَا تَكْفُرْ ﴿١٠٢﴾ ﴾

But neither of these two (angels) taught anyone (such things) till they had said, "We are only for trial, so disbelieve not (by learning this magic from us)."[2]

At the end of the verse He ﷻ said:

﴿ وَلَقَدْ عَلِمُوا لَمَنِ اشْتَرَاهُ مَا لَهُ فِي الْآخِرَةِ مِنْ خَلَاقٍ ﴿١٠٢﴾ ﴾

And indeed, they knew that the buyers of it (magic) would have no share in the Hereafter.[3]

[1] Sūrah al-Baqarah, 2:101-102
[2] Sūrah al-Baqarah, 2:102
[3] Sūrah al-Baqarah, 2:102

Having no share is proof that if the magician does not repent to Allāh then he will have no share in the Hereafter; and the person with no share in the Hereafter is a disbeliever. Thus, magic is disbelief. Based upon this, it is not permissible to pray behind the magician. Likewise, it is not permissible to believe in magic or to believe anything about it is valid. It is not permissible to practice it.

As for curing magic with other magic, the scholars have said this is not permissible because medicine can only come from that which is permissible and lawful. Allāh ﷻ did not place a cure for the Muslims in that which He prohibited them from. The Prophet ﷺ said:

تَدَاوَوْا وَلاَ تَدَاوَوْا بِحَرَامٍ

Use medicine but do not use medical treatment with the impermissible.[1]

Ibn Masūd ؓ said:

إِنَّ اللَّهَ لَمْ يَجْعَلْ شِفَاءَكُمْ فِيمَا حُرِّمَ عَلَيْكُمْ

Allāh does not put your cure in that which He has forbidden to you.[2]

[1] Sunan Abi Dāwūd, 3874
[2] Al-Bukhārī, 6/247

Magic is from the greatest matters which are forbidden, so it is not permissible to use it as a cure or medicine. You cannot use magic to remove magic. As for using magic to cure magic, the Prophet ﷺ said about this:

هُوَ مِنْ عَمَلِ الشَّيْطَانِ

This is from the works of Shayṭān.[1]

Hassan al-Basri said, "No one removes magic by using magic except for a magician."

Performing Magic Tricks on Social Media

QUESTION: There are some people who perform illusionary magic with fire and hitting themselves with hammers, and they place this on social media to show they can perform miracles. How can this be dealt with?

ANSWER: It is obligatory to disapprove of this and to prevent this from social media, this social media that we are in control over and have power over. As for the social media that we are not in control of, then we must ban it from our country. And if it occurs, we must request our rulers to remove it to protect the Muslims from its dangers and evil.

[1] Sunan Abi Dāwūd, 3868

Those Who Claim the Staff of Mūsa Was Magic

QUESTION: What is your advice to those who claim the staff of Mūsa ﷺ was magical?

ANSWER: This is disbelief in Allāh, the Exalted, if this person believes Mūsa ﷺ was a magician and that his staff was a magic tool. And with Allāh ﷻ refuge is sought. The staff of Mūsa was not magic; rather, it was a miracle from Allāh ﷻ. Whoever makes this statement must repent to Allāh, the Exalted, because this speech is vile and evil.

If this person does not believe Mūsa ﷺ was a magician, but he only says it blind following others then he has made a major mistake. And it is obligatory to stay far away from this terminology.

Seeking Assistance from Muslim Jinn

QUESTION: Some people are ignorant as it relates to the knowledge of recitation, so they seek help from the *jinn*. They say, "This is a Muslim *jinn*," and they ask the *jinn* where the magic is located. Is this permissible?

ANSWER: No one should seek help from the *jinn*, even if the *jinn* said he is Muslim. Perhaps he said he is Muslim, but he is lying in order to deceive the person. Therefore, this door must be closed at its root.

It is not permissible to seek help from the *jinn* because this opens the door to evil. It is not permissible to seek help from someone who is absent, whether they are a *jinn* or otherwise, whether they are Muslim or non-Muslim. It is only permissible to seek help from one who is present and has the ability to assist. As Allāh, the Exalted, said about Mūsa ﷺ:

﴿ فَاسْتَغَاثَهُ الَّذِي مِن شِيعَتِهِ عَلَى الَّذِي مِنْ عَدُوِّهِ ﴿١٥﴾ ﴾

The man of his (own) party asked him for help against his foe.[1]

This person is present and has the ability to help, so there is no prohibition in seeking his help in normal affairs.

Séances and Conjuring Spirits

QUESTION: What is the ruling on conjuring spirits? Is this a type of magic?

ANSWER: There is no doubt that conjuring spirits is a type of magic and soothsaying. These spirits are not the souls of the deceased as the people say. Rather, they are only the devils pretending to be the deceased. The devil will say, "I am the soul of so and so," while in reality it is a devil. Thus, this is not permissible.

[1] Sūrah al-Qaṣaṣ, 28:15

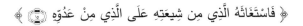

It is not possible to summon the souls of the deceased because they are in the grasp of Allāh ﷻ.

﴿ اللَّهُ يَتَوَفَّى الْأَنفُسَ حِينَ مَوْتِهَا وَالَّتِي لَمْ تَمُتْ فِي مَنَامِهَا ۖ فَيُمْسِكُ الَّتِي قَضَىٰ عَلَيْهَا الْمَوْتَ وَيُرْسِلُ الْأُخْرَىٰ إِلَىٰ أَجَلٍ مُّسَمًّى ﴿٤٢﴾ ﴾

It is Allāh Who takes away the souls at the time of their death, and those that die not during their sleep. He keeps those (souls) for which He has ordained death and sends the rest for a term appointed.[1]

The souls do not travel about as they allege, except by the disposal of Allāh ﷻ. Therefore, conjuring spirits is false, and it is a type of magic and soothsaying.

Sacrificing an Animal for the New Home

QUESTION: When some people want to build a home, they sacrifice a sheep or lamb in the home, saying, "This is to solidify the foundation."

ANSWER: This is *shirk*. This is associating partners with Allāh ﷻ and sacrificing for the *jinn*. They sacrifice the animal on the threshold of the house. Or before the company starts a contract they sacrifice the animal before starting the transaction. They say. "This will benefit the

[1] Sūrah az-Zumar, 39:42

project." This is associating partners with Allāh ﷻ because it is sacrificing for the *jinn* and putting faith in the *jinn*. It is the *jinn* who commanded them to do this and whispered to them to believe this would benefit them. Whoever sacrifices for other than Allāh ﷻ has committed *shirk*. The Prophet ﷺ said:

لَعَنَ اللَّهُ مَنْ ذَبَحَ لِغَيْرِ اللَّهِ

Allāh has cursed the one who sacrifices for other than Allāh.[1]

Allāh, the Exalted, said:

﴿ قُلْ إِنَّ صَلَاتِي وَنُسُكِي وَمَحْيَايَ وَمَمَاتِي لِلَّهِ رَبِّ الْعَالَمِينَ ١٦٢ ﴾

Say (O Muḥammad): "Verily, my prayer, my sacrifice, my living, and my dying are for Allāh, the Lord of all that exists."[2]

Sacrifice is slaughtering the animal, and it has been mentioned alongside the prayer. Then just as the person cannot pray to other than Allāh ﷻ, he cannot sacrifice for other than Allāh. Allāh, the Exalted, said:

---

[1] Al-Adab al-Mufrad, 17

[2] Sūrah al-'An'ām, 6:162

﴿ فَصَلِّ لِرَبِّكَ وَانْحَرْ ۝ ﴾

Therefore, turn in prayer to your Lord and sacrifice (to Him only).[1]

Sacrifice is worship and worship is the exclusive right of Allāh ﷻ alone.

Astrology Versus Astronomy

QUESTION: Is astrology considered knowing the movements of the stars throughout the year, months and days; and knowing when the rain will fall and the like?

ANSWER: This is not considered astrology. This is permissible knowledge. Allāh created the sun and the moon for us to keep account of time. Allāh, the Exalted, said:

﴿ هُوَ الَّذِي جَعَلَ الشَّمْسَ ضِيَاءً وَالْقَمَرَ نُورًا وَقَدَّرَهُ مَنَازِلَ لِتَعْلَمُوا عَدَدَ السِّنِينَ وَالْحِسَابَ ۝ ﴾

It is He who made the sun a shining light and the moon a derived light and determined for it phases -

[1] Sūrah al-Kawthar, 108:2

that you may know the number of years and account [of time].[1]

This knowledge is known as astronomy. Al-Khatabi said, "As for the knowledge of the stars which is known by looking at them and gathering information to know the settings and direction of the prayer, then this is not included in the prohibition."

Using the stars for directional purposes is not prohibited. Allāh, the Exalted, said:

﴿ وَعَلَامَاتٍ ۚ وَبِالنَّجْمِ هُمْ يَهْتَدُونَ ﴿١٦﴾ ﴾

And landmarks. And by the stars, they (mankind) guide themselves.[2]

Al-Bukhārī said that Qatada said, "Allāh ﷻ created the stars for three purposes: beautification of the sky, missiles to shoot at the devils, and signs to guide the travelers. Thus, whoever seeks other than this has erred and delved into a matter he has no knowledge of.

Shaykh Sulaymān ibn Abdullah said, "This is extracted from the Qur'ān, from the statement of Allāh, the Exalted:

﴿ وَلَقَدْ زَيَّنَّا السَّمَاءَ الدُّنْيَا بِمَصَابِيحَ وَجَعَلْنَاهَا رُجُومًا لِّلشَّيَاطِينِ ﴿٥﴾ ﴾

---

[1] Sūrah Yūnus, 10:5

[2] Sūrah an-Naḥl, 16:16

And indeed, We have adorned the nearest heaven with lamps, and We have made such lamps (as) missiles to drive away the devils.[1]

And His statement:

﴿ وَعَلَامَاتٍ ۚ وَبِالنَّجْمِ هُمْ يَهْتَدُونَ ﴾

And landmarks. And by the stars, they (mankind) guide themselves.[2]

The word "landmarks" refers to those signs within the towns.[3]

As for knowing exactly when it will rain this is not possible, because knowing exactly when the rain will fall is from the matters of the unseen only known to Allāh ﷻ. Attaching the rainfall to the movement of the stars is to seek rain based upon the weather and this is from the affairs of pre-Islāmic ignorance.[4]

---

[1] Sūrah al-Mulk, 67:5

[2] Sūrah an-Naḥl, 16:16

[3] Taysir al Aziz al Hamid in explaining the *Book of Tawhīd*, page 443

[4] Translator's note: Shaykh Uthaymīn was asked, "Is twenty-four-hour weather reporting such as we have now fortune-telling?" He replied, "The answer is no, because it is also based on scientific data which is describing climatic conditions, because climatic conditions have to do with precise measurements that are known to them. Thus, they may predict that certain conditions are likely to produce rain or not. That is like the primitive predication that we make when we see clouds forming, and thunder and lightning and

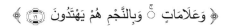

As for knowing the time for seeding the crops, this returns to knowledge of the seasons. This knowledge can be known through calculations. And Allāh ﷻ knows best.

Palm Reading, Cup Reading and Horoscopes

QUESTION: What is your view on cup reading, palm reading and what is known as horoscopes which are circulated in the newspaper?

ANSWER: All of that is soothsaying. Cup reading, palm reading and horoscopes which are circulated in the newspaper claim knowledge of the unseen. Thus, it is soothsaying.

Soothsaying is a category of magic. Soothsaying, magic, and fortunetelling are all types of falsehood that claim knowledge of the unseen. This deceives the people and corrupts their *'āqīdah.*

Claiming Knowledge of What Occurred Millions of Years Ago

QUESTION: We hear some people saying, "This has been known or this occurred over one hundred million years ago, or one hundred

---

thick clouds, and we say, 'It is going to rain soon.' What matters is that what points to physical phenomena is not knowledge of the unseen, even if some of the common folk think that these things are matters of the unseen and say that believing in them is like believing in fortune-telling." (*al-Qawl al-Mufeed*, the explanation of the *Book of Tawhīd*.)

and fifty million years ago." Is this statement permissible? Is it possible to make such a calculation? And are there millions of years between us and Adam ﷺ?

Answer: Claiming knowledge of what occurred millions of years ago is delving into matters without any proof or evidence. It is not permissible to speak about the unseen matters of the past except with authentic proof from the Book of Allāh ﷻ, the Sunnah of His Messenger ﷺ, or verified information. No one knows the past generations except for Allāh ﷻ. The Exalted said:

﴿ وَكَمْ أَهْلَكْنَا مِنَ الْقُرُونِ مِن بَعْدِ نُوحٍ ﴿١٧﴾ ﴾

And how many generations have We destroyed after Nuh![1]

And the Exalted said:

﴿ أَلَمْ يَأْتِكُمْ نَبَأُ الَّذِينَ مِن قَبْلِكُمْ قَوْمِ نُوحٍ وَعَادٍ وَثَمُودَ ۛ وَالَّذِينَ مِن بَعْدِهِمْ ۛ لَا يَعْلَمُهُمْ إِلَّا اللَّهُ ﴿٩﴾ ﴾

Has not the news reached you, of those before you, the people of Nuh, and 'Ad, and Thamud? And those after them? None knows them but Allāh.[2]

---

[1] Sūrah Al-'Isrā', 17:17

[2] Sūrah 'Ibrāhīm, 14:9

That which is written on the internet and found in some books, stating that some artifact is millions of years old is conjecture, fabrication, and speaking without knowledge.

THE EVIL EYE, ENVY, WHISPERS AND AMULETS

Unintentional Evil Eye

QUESTION: If the envier afflicts someone with the evil eye unintentionally is there anything upon him to do? Is there any treatment for the envier and the envied to take to lessen the effect of the evil eye or completely remove it?

ANSWER: The eye is real, as is mentioned in the *ḥadīth*. And it is from the amazing creations of Allāh ﷻ that He placed harm in the look of individuals, which affects those whom the glance falls upon. The Prophet ﷺ said:

الْعَيْنُ حَقٌّ

The eye is real.[1]

[1] Muslim, 4/1719

There is a prescribed treatment for the one who gives the eye and for the one who is affected by it. As for the person who gives the eye and he is afraid he will harm what he looked at; he repels the evil of his look by saying:

اللهم بارِك عليه

O Allāh bless it.

The Prophet ﷺ said to ʿĀmir ibn Rabiʿah (عَامِرُ بْنُ رَبِيعَةَ), when he put the eye on Saḥl ibn Ḥanīf (سَهْلَ بْنَ حُنَيْفٍ):

أَلاَّ بَرَّكْتَ

Would you not have invoked blessings upon him?

This means he should have said, "O Allāh bless him."

If the person fears he will harm someone with his look he should say, "O Allāh bless him." It is likewise recommended to say:

مَا شَاءَ اللَّهُ لاَ قُوَّةَ إِلاَّ بِاللَّهِ

What Allāh has willed, there is no power except with Allāh.

It has been narrated from Hishām ibn ʿUrwa (هِشام بن عُرْوَة), from his father, that he saw something that amazed him. He said, "What Allāh ﷻ has willed, there is no power except with Allāh."

So, if the person giving the look adheres to this supplication, then it will repel the harm by the permission of Allāh ﷻ.

If the person gives someone the eye purposefully, he earns a sin for doing so, because he is transgressing the person with this. Such that the scholars, may Allāh ﷻ have mercy upon them, have said that if someone intends to kill someone with his eye and he confesses to that, then retaliation is taken upon him, because this is considered an intentionally killing.

As for the person afflicted by the eye, then he utilizes the *ruqya* used by Jibrīl on the Prophet ﷺ. And this is to say:

بِسْمِ اللَّهِ أَرْقِيكَ، مِنْ كُلِّ شَيْءٍ يُؤْذِيكَ، مِنْ شَرِّ كُلِّ نَفْسٍ أَوْ عَيْنِ حَاسِدٍ،
اللَّهُ يَشْفِيكَ بِسْمِ اللَّهِ أَرْقِيكَ

In the Name of Allāh I perform ruqya upon you from everything that harms you, and from every evil soul or envious eye; may Allāh heal you. In the Name of Allāh I perform ruqya upon you.[1]

The person can say this supplication himself or one of his brothers can say it for him and blow lightly on him. This will repel the eye with the permission of Allāh. And Allāh ﷻ knows best.

[1] Muslim 4/1718 from the *ḥadīth* of Abu Saīd, ﷺ.

The eye can likewise be treated with washing. The person who gave the eye washes the inside of his trousers then the water is poured over the person afflicted with the eye. This was directed by the Prophet ﷺ.[1]

Cure from Evil Whispers

QUESTION: What is the ruling concerning the whispers of the soul? If a person's soul whispers filthy things to him, and he is severely harmed and afraid due to these whispers—keeping in mind that he does not believe in nor work according to these whispers, but the whispers are beyond his control—will he be taken to account for them?

ANSWER: The whispers don't harm the person and he will not be taken to account for what he does not speak on or act upon. It is mentioned in the *ḥadīth*:

إِنَّ اللَّهَ تَجَاوَزَ لأُمَّتِي مَا حَدَّثَتْ بِهِ أَنْفُسَهَا مَا لَمْ يَتَكَلَّمُوا أَوْ يَعْمَلُوا بِهِ

Verily Allāh has pardoned my nation the evil promptings which arise within their hearts as long as

[1] Aḥmad, 3/486

they did not speak about them or did not act upon them.[1]

The whispers which enter upon man are from Shayṭān. He wants to make the Muslim sad with these whispers and distract him from the obedience of Allāh ﷻ. Thus, it is upon the Muslim to seek refuge in Allāh ﷻ from the Shayṭān, and he should not look toward these whispers or give them any consideration. If he does this; these whispers will not harm him.

QUESTION: I am a young man who the Shayṭān whispers to sometimes. What can I do to repel these whispers?

ANSWER: The whispers of Shayṭān are repelled by seeking refuge in Allāh ﷻ from the Shayṭān and not paying attention to these whispers. The whispers will not harm the individual if he does not speak with them.

The Muslim must reject them, ignore them and seek refuge in Allāh ﷻ from the accursed devil.

Hanging Amulets on the Necks of Children

QUESTION: What is the ruling on hanging amulets on the necks of children if the amulets contain verses of the Qur'ān or Prophetic supplications?

---

[1] Saḥiḥ Muslim, 127

ANSWER: The correct statement from the scholars is that it is not permissible to hang these amulets, and this is due to a number of reasons.

1. There is no evidence to prove it is permissible. Therefore, the principle is that it is prohibited due to the general prohibition of hanging amulets, such as the statement of the Prophet ﷺ:

مَنْ تَعَلَّقَ تَمِيمَةً ، فَلَا أَتَمَّ اللَّهُ لَهُ

Whoever wears an amulet, may Allāh not fulfill his need.[1]

2. Permitting the hanging of these amulets will be a means to allow amulets that contain shirk and impermissible words.
3. Permitting the hanging of these amulets is a means by which the Qur'ān will be belittled and exposed to being taken inside inappropriate places. Likewise, hanging these amulets on the children will expose them to filth.

Performing *ruqya* directly on the sick individual and reciting the Qur'ān over him suffices. And all praises belong to Allāh ﷻ.

---

[1] Aḥmad, 16951

Selling Necklaces with Qur'ānic Verses Written on Them

QUESTION: We see some necklaces with Qur'ānic verses written on them. Is it permissible to buy, sell and wear them?

ANSWER: It is not permissible to buy, sell or wear these necklaces which have Qur'ānic verses written on them. This is because it is belittlement of the Qur'ān and could be used as an amulet that the sick believe will be a means to heal them. The Prophet ﷺ has prohibited wearing amulets, and this prohibition is general to include necklaces that contain Qur'ānic verses or otherwise. And Allāh ﷻ knows best.

Bracelets and Necklaces Made from Animal Hair

QUESTION: We notice some people wearing bracelets around their necks and wrists, decorated with specific paint or strings made of animal hair. They believe these bracelets protection from the harm that the *jinn* could bring. Is this permissible?

ANSWER: As for wearing these bracelets, and tying strings made of hair when the person believes these things in and of themselves protect the person who wears them from harm, then this is major shirk which removes the person from the fold of Islām. This is because he believes these things bring about benefit and protect against harm, and no one has the ability to do this except for Allāh, the Exalted.

If the person believes Allāh ﷻ is the One who brings about benefit and protects against harm, and these things are merely a means, then this is impermissible and minor shirk which leads to major shirk. This is because he believes these things are a means, but Allāh did not make them a means. Allāh ﷻ has placed a means for curing in medicine and legislated *ruqya*, and these things are not permissible medicine or legislated *ruqya*.

Shaykh Muḥammad ibn 'Abdul-Wahhāb placed a chapter in *Kitab at-Tawḥīd* surrounding this subject. He entitled the chapter, "The Shirk of Wearing Rings and Strings to Repel or Remove Harm". From the evidence of its prohibition is that he mentioned the *ḥadīth* of 'Imran ibn Ḥussein ﷺ.

أَنَّ النَّبِيَّ . صلى الله عليه وسلم . رَأَى رَجُلاً فِي يَدِهِ حَلْقَةٌ مِنْ صُفْرٍ فَقَالَ " مَا هَذِهِ الْحَلْقَةُ ". قَالَ هَذِهِ مِنَ الْوَاهِنَةِ . قَالَ " انْزِعْهَا فَإِنَّهَا لاَ تَزِيدُكَ إِلاَّ وَهْنًا

The Prophet ﷺ saw a man with a brass ring on his hand. He said: "What is this ring?" He said: "It is for weakness." He said: "Take it off, for it will only increase you in weakness[1]."

[1] Collected by Aḥmad 4/445, and authenticated by al-Hakim 4/216

Huḍaifah saw a man with string in his hand to protect against sickness. He cut the string and then he recited the verse:

﴿ وَمَا يُؤْمِنُ أَكْثَرُهُم بِاللَّهِ إِلَّا وَهُم مُّشْرِكُونَ ﴿١٠٦﴾ ﴾

And most of them believe not in Allāh except that they attribute partners unto Him.[1]

If he believes these items protect against the evil of the *jinn*, then nothing can protect against their evil except for Allāh ﷻ. Allāh, the Exalted, said:

﴿ وَإِمَّا يَنزَغَنَّكَ مِنَ الشَّيْطَانِ نَزْغٌ فَاسْتَعِذْ بِاللَّهِ ۚ إِنَّهُ سَمِيعٌ عَلِيمٌ ﴿٢٠٠﴾ ﴾

And if an evil whisper comes to you from Shayṭān then seek refuge with Allāh. Verily, He is All-Hearer, All-Knower.[2]

Writing Supplications for the Newborn

QUESTION: When one of us has a child, we write a supplication for the newborn from the Noble Qur'ān and hang it on his shoulder or neck. And it appears this give the baby relief. Is this permissible?

[1] Sūrah Yūsuf, 12:106

[2] Sūrah al-'A'rāf, 7:200

ANSWER: Hanging "words of protection" on adults or children is not permissible because these are considered amulets, and the Prophet ﷺ forbade hanging amulets.

If the amulets contain imaginary things, talismans, unknown words, the names of devils, *jinn*, or unknown names; then this is impermissible. This is because all of this damages the *'āqīdah* and leads to absolute *shirk* according to the consensus of the Muslims.

If the amulet contains the Qur'ān or legislated supplications, then the most correct statement from the scholars is that this is also impermissible. This is because if this door is open the people will expand into other areas and begin to place things in the amulet which are *ḥaram*. This is from one standpoint.

The other standpoint is that attaching the Qur'ān to children is belittlement of the Qur'ān. This is because a child will not be careful not to enter the bathroom and filthy places while having the Qur'ān attached to him. This is belittlement of the Speech of Allāh ﷻ; thus, this is not permissible.

Saying that it brings the child ease or it cures him is not proof that this thing is permissible. The child receiving ease or a cure after hanging an amulet on him could just coincide with his decreed healing, while they believe it is connected to the amulet. Or this could be a method in which they are gradually deceived until they fall into something more evil than that. Receiving the desired result after using these means is not proof that these means are permissible.

TRUSTING IN ALLĀH

What Does Reliance Upon Allāh Mean?

QUESTION: What is the meaning of "reliance upon Allāh" and what is its reality? Is reliance upon Allāh ﷻ only during times of hardship or is it during all times? What is the answer to those who believe reliance upon Allāh means not taking the necessary means?

ANSWER: The word "*tawwakul*" (reliance) in the language means entrusting and depending. Thus, reliance on Allāh ﷻ means depending upon Allāh, the Exalted, and entrusting all affairs to Him.

This is an obligation which must be done sincerely for Allāh ﷻ. Allāh, the Exalted, said:

﴿ وَعَلَى اللَّهِ فَتَوَكَّلُوا إِن كُنتُم مُّؤْمِنِينَ ﴿٢٣﴾ ﴾

And upon Allāh place your trust if you are indeed believers.[1]

[1] Sūrah al-Mā'idah, 5:23

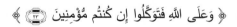

And the Exalted said:

﴿ إِن كُنتُمْ آمَنتُم بِاللَّهِ فَعَلَيْهِ تَوَكَّلُوا إِن كُنتُم مُّسْلِمِينَ ﴿٨٤﴾ ﴾

If you have believed in Allāh, then put your trust in Him if you are Muslims.[1]

Thus, Allāh ﷻ made reliance upon Him a condition for faith and Islām, and this proves the importance of it. It is the most comprehensive form of worship and the highest, noblest, greatest station of monotheism because it brings about righteous actions.

Reliance upon Allāh ﷻ is in all matters and not just some situations.

Reliance upon Allāh ﷻ does not mean abandoning the means because Allāh commanded us to rely upon Him, and He commanded us to utilize the means. Allāh, the Exalted, said:

﴿ وَأَعِدُّوا لَهُم مَّا اسْتَطَعْتُم مِّن قُوَّةٍ ﴿٦٠﴾ ﴾

And make ready against them all you can of power.[2]

And Allah, the Exalted, said:

﴿ خُذُوا حِذْرَكُمْ ﴿٧١﴾ ﴾

[1] Sūrah Yūnus, 10:84

[2] Sūrah al-'Anfāl, 8:60

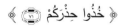

Take your precautions.[1]

The individual takes the necessary means, but he does not rely upon the means to bring about the required results.

The Prophet ﷺ was the greatest in terms of relying upon Allāh ﷻ, and yet he would carry a weapon, wear a shield and place a helmet on his head.[2]

Some people used to go to perform Hajj without taking the necessary provisions, and thus they became dependent upon others. They considered themselves relying upon Allāh ﷻ by not taking provisions. Thus, Allāh ﷻ sent down the verse:

﴿ وَتَزَوَّدُوا فَإِنَّ خَيْرَ الزَّادِ التَّقْوَىٰ ﴿١٩٧﴾ ﴾

And take provisions, but indeed, the best provision is fear of Allāh.[3]

For this reason, it is said that relying upon the means is *shirk*, while abandoning the means is to disparage the legislation. Don't make you reliance weakness and do not make your weakness reliance. Verily, paradise is not obtained except by means, and these means are righteous actions. And Allāh ﷻ knows best.

[1] Sūrah an-Nisā', 4:71
[2] Zād al-Mā'ād, 1/130-133
[3] Sūrah al-Baqarah, 2:197

How to Rely Upon Allāh

QUESTION: How can a person become someone who relies upon Allāh?

ANSWER: The individual becomes someone who relies by being trustful in his reliance upon Allāh ﷻ; such that he knows that all good lies in the Hand of Allāh, the Exalted, and He is the One who controls all the affairs. The Prophet ﷺ said to 'Abdullah ibn 'Abbas:

يا غلام إني أعلمك كلمات: "احفظ الله يحفظك، احفظ الله تجده تجاهك، إذا سألت فاسأل الله ، وإذا استعنت فاستعن بالله، واعلم: أن الأمة لو اجتمعت على أن ينفعوك بشيء، لم ينفعوك إلا بشيء قد كتبه الله لك، وإن اجتمعوا على أن يضروك بشيء، لم يضروك بشيء إلا بشيء قد كتبه الله عليك

"O young boy, be mindful of Allāh and He will protect you. Be mindful of Allāh and you will find Him in front of you. If you ask, ask of Allāh; if you seek help, seek help from Allāh. And remember that if all the people gather to benefit you, they will not be able to benefit you except that which Allāh had foreordained (for you); and if all of them gather to do harm to you, they will not be able to afflict you with any

thing other than that which Allāh had pre-destined against you.[1]

With this belief and creed. the person will be one who relies upon Allāh ﷻ and does not look toward anyone else.

The reality of reliance upon Allāh ﷻ does not negate taking the necessary means which Allāh, the Exalted, has made as a means. Rather, utilizing the necessary means which Allāh ﷻ has made—whether it be a religious means or a tangible means—this is from the completeness of reliance upon Allāh, and from complete belief in the wisdom of Allāh ﷻ. This is because Allāh, the Exalted, has made a means for everything. The Prophet ﷺ —the best of those who rely upon Allāh ﷻ—used to wear a shield during war. He protected himself from the cold, and he ate and drank in order to stay alive and nourish his body. During the battle of 'Uḥud he wore two shields.[2].

Those who believe reliance upon Allāh ﷻ is by abandoning the means and relying upon Allāh have fallen into error. The One who commanded us to rely upon Him has infinite wisdom in His decree and legislation. Thus, He gave us means by which we can obtain the desired results.

---

[1] Aḥmad, 1/293

[2] Zād al-Mā'ād, 1/130-133

A person might say, "I will rely upon Allāh with regard to obtaining provision. I will remain in my home and not seek provision!" We say to him this is not correct and this is not true reliance upon Allāh ﷻ. The One who commanded us to rely upon Him said:

﴿ هُوَ الَّذِي جَعَلَ لَكُمُ الْأَرْضَ ذَلُولًا فَامْشُوا فِي مَنَاكِبِهَا وَكُلُوا مِن رِّزْقِهِ ۖ وَإِلَيْهِ النُّشُورُ ﴿١٥﴾ ﴾

He it is, Who has made the earth subservient to you, so walk in the path thereof and eat of His provision, and to Him will be the Resurrection.[1]

Someone might say, "I will rely upon Allāh in having a child, or I will rely upon Allāh in getting a wife, but I will not seek marriage or engagement!" If someone says this, the people would consider him foolish, because to do such negates what the wisdom of Allāh ﷻ necessitates.

If someone were to take poison and say, "I will place my trust in Allāh that this poison will not harm me!" This person does not rely upon Allāh ﷻ in reality, because the One who commanded us to rely upon Him said:

﴿ وَلَا تَقْتُلُوا أَنفُسَكُمْ ۚ إِنَّ اللَّهَ كَانَ بِكُمْ رَحِيمًا ﴿٢٩﴾ ﴾

[1] Sūrah al-Mulk, 67:15

And do not kill yourselves. Surely, Allāh is Most Merciful to you.[1]

The means that Allāh, the Exalted, has placed as means does not negate reliance upon Allāh ﷻ; rather, it is the completeness of reliance upon Allāh. To expose yourself to destruction is not considered relying upon Allāh ﷻ, rather it is in contrast to what Allāh has commanded and it is prohibited.

How to Attach Your Heart to Allāh

QUESTION: What are the specific means by which the individual can attach his heart to Allāh, the Exalted?

ANSWER: The specific means by which the individual can attach his heart to Allāh ﷻ is by increasing his recitation of the Noble Qur'ān, reflecting upon Allāh's favors, fearing the punishment of Allāh ﷻ, hoping for His reward, and increasing his remembrance of Allāh. Allāh, the Exalted, said:

﴿ الَّذِينَ آمَنُوا وَتَطْمَئِنُّ قُلُوبُهُم بِذِكْرِ اللَّهِ ۗ أَلَا بِذِكْرِ اللَّهِ تَطْمَئِنُّ الْقُلُوبُ ﴿٢٨﴾ ﴾

---

[1] Sūrah an-Nisā', 4:29

Those who believe, and whose hearts find rest in the remembrance of Allāh, verily, in the remembrance of Allāh do hearts find rest.[1]

Likewise, some specific means to attach your heart to Allāh ﷻ is by looking at His universal signs and reflecting upon them. Allāh, the Exalted, said:

﴿ إِنَّ فِي خَلْقِ السَّمَاوَاتِ وَالْأَرْضِ وَاخْتِلَافِ اللَّيْلِ وَالنَّهَارِ لَآيَاتٍ لِّأُولِي الْأَلْبَابِ ﴿١٩٠﴾ الَّذِينَ يَذْكُرُونَ اللَّهَ قِيَامًا وَقُعُودًا وَعَلَىٰ جُنُوبِهِمْ وَيَتَفَكَّرُونَ فِي خَلْقِ السَّمَاوَاتِ وَالْأَرْضِ رَبَّنَا مَا خَلَقْتَ هَٰذَا بَاطِلًا سُبْحَانَكَ فَقِنَا عَذَابَ النَّارِ ﴿١٩١﴾ ﴾

Verily! In the creation of the heavens and the earth, and in the alternation of night and day, there are indeed signs for men of understanding. Those who remember Allāh standing, sitting, and lying down on their sides, and think deeply about the creation of the heavens and the earth, (saying): "Our Lord! You have not created (all) this without purpose, glory to You! (Exalted be You above all that they associate with You

[1] Sūrah ar-Ra'd, 13:28

as partners). Give us salvation from the torment of the Fire."[1]

Storing Food in the Home

QUESTION: Does buying food and storing it in the home during these days and times negate reliance upon Allāh, the Exalted?

ANSWER: There is no problem with buying food and storing it the homes for the purpose of consumption because this is taking care of a need. The only exception is if this harms others by creating a shortage of merchandise, such that the people are not able to acquire the product or the price is inflated.

[1] Sūrah 'Āli 'Imrān, 3:190-191

Translator's Appendix: Qur'ānic Verses and Supplications to Remove Magic

In his explanation of *Kitab at-Tawḥīd*[1], Shaykh Saliḥ al-Fawzān mentioned that magic is removed by reciting verses from the Book of Allah, the Exalted, and by supplications.

Ruqyah is performed by reciting verses from the Qur'ān, the Book of Allah ﷻ, upon the person afflicted with magic.

Al-Fāṭiḥah should be recited upon them. This is the greatest *ruqyah.*

The verses which mention magic and invalidating magic should be recited; such as the statement of the Exalted in Sūrah al-'A'rāf:

﴿ وَأَوْحَيْنَا إِلَى مُوسَى أَنْ أَلْقِ عَصَاكَ فَإِذَا هِيَ تَلْقَفُ مَا يَأْفِكُونَ ﴿١١٧﴾
فَوَقَعَ الْحَقُّ وَبَطَلَ مَا كَانُوا يَعْمَلُونَ ﴿١١٨﴾ فَغُلِبُوا هُنَالِكَ وَانقَلَبُوا
صَاغِرِينَ ﴿١١٩﴾ وَأُلْقِيَ السَّحَرَةُ سَاجِدِينَ ﴿١٢٠﴾ قَالُوا آمَنَّا بِرَبِّ الْعَالَمِينَ
﴿١٢١﴾ رَبِّ مُوسَى وَهَارُونَ ﴿١٢٢﴾ ﴾

[1] Volume 1, page 380

And We inspired Mūsa (saying): "Throw your stick," and behold! It swallowed up straight away all the falsehoods which they showed. Thus, truth was confirmed, and all that they did was made of no effect. So they were defeated there and then, and were returned disgraced. And the magicians fell down in prostration. They said: "We believe in the Lord of all that exists; the Lord of Mūsa and Hārūn.

[Sūrah al-'A'rāf 7: 117-122]

And in Sūrah Yūnus:

﴿ فَلَمَّا أَلْقَوْاْ قَالَ مُوسَى مَا جِئْتُم بِهِ السِّحْرُ إِنَّ اللّهَ سَيُبْطِلُهُ إِنَّ اللّهَ
لاَ يُصْلِحُ عَمَلَ الْمُفْسِدِينَ ﴿٨١﴾ وَيُحِقُّ اللّهُ الْحَقَّ بِكَلِمَاتِهِ وَلَوْ كَرِهَ
الْمُجْرِمُونَ ﴿٨٢﴾ ﴾

Then when they had cast down, Mūsa said: "What you have brought is sorcery, Allāh will surely make it of no effect. Verily, Allāh does not set right the work of al-Mufsidun (the evil-doers, etc.). And Allāh will establish and make apparent the truth by His Words, however much the Mujrimun (criminals, disbelievers, etc.) may hate it."

[Sūrah Yūnus: 10:81, 82]

And in Sūrah Ṭāhā:

﴿ وَأَلْقِ مَا فِي يَمِينِكَ تَلْقَفْ مَا صَنَعُوا إِنَّمَا صَنَعُوا كَيْدُ سَاحِرٍ وَلَا يُفْلِحُ السَّاحِرُ حَيْثُ أَتَى ﴿٦٩﴾ فَأُلْقِيَ السَّحَرَةُ سُجَّدًا قَالُوا آمَنَّا بِرَبِّ هَارُونَ وَمُوسَى ﴿٧٠﴾ ﴾

"And throw that which is in your right hand! It will swallow up that which they have made. That which they have made is only a magician's trick, and the magician will never be successful, no matter whatever amount (of skill) he may attain." So the magicians fell down prostrate. They said: "We believe in the Lord of Hārūn and Mūsa."

[Sūrah Ṭāhā 20:69-70]

These verses from Sūrah al-'A'rāf, Sūrah Yūnus, and Sūrah Ṭāhā, should be recited by the one performing the *ruqyah* upon the afflicted person. They should be recited with an attentive heart, reliance upon Allāh, the Exalted, while having a good thought about Allāh, and believing that Allāh ﷻ will heal this sick person.

As for the person being read upon, he should also have this *'āqīdah*. Thus, he hopes for the cure from Allāh ﷻ, he puts his trust in Allāh, the Exalted, he relies upon Him, and he believes that the speech of Allāh ﷻ contains the cure.

If they turn to Allāh in this manner, and both the person reciting and the person being recited upon place their trust in Allāh ﷻ, they will achieve the desired result, and there is no doubt about it.

SUPPLICATIONS TO REMOVE MAGIC

أَعِيذُكَ بِكَلِمَاتِ اللهِ التَّامَّاتِ مِنْ شَرِّ مَا خَلَقَ

I seek refuge for you in the perfect words of Allāh from the evil of which He created.[1]

أَعِيذُكَ بِكَلِمَاتِ اللهِ التَّامَّةِ مِنْ كُلِّ شَيْطَانٍ وَهَامَّةٍ وَمِنْ كُلِّ عَيْنٍ لَامَّةٍ

I seek refuge for you with the perfect words of Allāh from every devil and from poisonous pests and from every evil, harmful, envious eye.[2]

أَعُوذُ بِكَلِمَاتِ اللهِ التَّامَّاتِ الَّتِي لَا يُجَاوِزُهُنَّ بَرٌّ وَلَا فَاجِرٌ مِنْ شَرِّ مَا خَلَقَ وَذَرَأَ وَبَرَأَ وَمِنْ شَرِّ مَا يَنْزِلُ مِنَ السَّمَاءِ وَمِنْ شَرِّ مَا يَعْرُجُ فِيهَا وَمِنْ شَرِّ مَا ذَرَأَ فِي الْأَرْضِ وَمِنْ شَرِّ مَا يَخْرُجُ مِنْهَا وَمِنْ شَرِّ فِتَنِ اللَّيْلِ وَالنَّهَارِ وَمِنْ شَرِّ كُلِّ طَارِقٍ إِلَّا طَارِقًا يَطْرُقُ بِخَيْرٍ يَا رَحْمَن

---

[1] Saḥiḥ Muslim, 2708

[2] Saḥiḥ al-Bukhārī, 3371

I seek refuge in the perfect words of Allāh, which neither the good person nor the corrupt can exceed, from the evil of what He created, fashioned and formed, from the evil which descends from the sky and from the evil which ascends to it, and from the evil He created in the earth and from the evil which comes out of it, and from the evil of the ordeals of the night and the day, and from the evil of every visitor, except the visitor who comes knocking with good, O Most Merciful.[1]

بِسْمِ اللَّهِ أَرْقِيكَ ، مِنْ كُلِّ دَاءٍ يُؤْذِيكَ ، وَمِنْ شَرِّ كُلِّ نَفْسٍ وَعَيْنٍ حَاسِدٍ،

اللَّهُ يَشْفِيكَ

In the Name of Allāh I perform *ruqyah* over you, from every disease which harms you, and from the evil of every soul, and envious eye, may Allāh cure you.[2]

بِسْمِ اللَّهِ أَذْهِبْ الْبَأْسَ رَبَّ النَّاسِ وَاشْفِه أَنْتَ الشَّافِي لاَ شِفَاءَ إِلاَّ شِفَاؤُك

شِفَاءً لاَ يُغَادِرُ سَقَمًا

[1] This is a longer version of the *ḥadīth* cited by Shaykh bin Bāz, collected in *Muwatta Imām Mālik*, 1742

[2] Sunan Ibn Majah, 3652

In the Name of Allāh, remove the hardship, O Lord of the people, heal him, You are the Healer, there is no cure except for Your cure; that cure which leaves behind no illness.[1]

رَبَّنَا اللَّهَ الَّذِي فِي السَّمَاءِ ، تَقَدَّسَ اسْمُكَ ، أَمْرُكَ فِي السَّمَاءِ وَالْأَرْضِ ، كَمَا رَحْمَتُكَ فِي السَّمَاءِ اجْعَلْ رَحْمَتَكَ فِي الْأَرْضِ ، اغْفِرْ لَنَا حُوبَنَا وَخَطَايَانَا ، أَنْتَ رَبُّ الطَّيِّبِينَ ، أَنْزِلْ رَحْمَةً مِنْ رَحْمَتِكَ ، وَشِفَاءً مِنْ شِفَائِكَ عَلَى هَذَا الْمَرْضِ

Our Lord is Allāh, the One who is above the heavens, blessed is Your Name. Your command is in the heavens and the earth. Just as Your mercy is in the heavens, make Your mercy upon the earth. Forgive us our sins and errors. You are the Lord of the pious, send down a mercy from Your mercy, and a healing from Your healing upon this sick person.[2]

---

[1] Saḥiḥ Muslim, 2191

[2] Sunan Abi Dāwūd, 3892